THE CHURCH

GEORGE STEWART

Author of

History of Religious Education in Connecticut
Protestant Europe: Its Crisis and Outlook
Can I Teach My Child Religion?
and other books

Price 50 cents

HAZEN BOOKS ON RELIGION
The Edward W. Hazen Foundation, Inc.

Distributed by
ASSOCIATION PRESS
347 Madison Avenue
NEW YORK

A Note about
The Hazen Books on Religion

THIS is the seventh volume of a series of little books called the *Hazen Books on Religion*. The purpose of the series is to present simply, compactly, and inexpensively a number of the best available interpretations of the Christian philosophy as a guide to Christian living today.

The series is sponsored by the Edward W. Hazen Foundation. The responsibility for selecting the titles and authors and for planning the manufacture and distribution of the volumes rests with the following committee: John C. Bennett (chairman), Wilbur Davies, Georgia Harkness, S. M. Keeny, Benson Y. Landis, Mrs. W. W. Rockwell, William L. Savage, George Stewart, Henry P. Van Dusen, and E. A. Yarrow. The responsibility for the subject matter of the volumes rests with the authors alone.

The following volumes in this series have already been published.

Christianity—and Our World. By John C. Bennett. (Six printings)
Jesus. By Mary Ely Lyman. (Four printings)
God. By Walter Horton. (Three printings)
Religious Living. By Georgia Harkness. (Three printings)
Toward a World Christian Fellowship. By Kenneth Scott Latourette.
Prayer and Worship. By Douglas Steere.
The Church. By George Stewart.

The titles listed below will follow at intervals of several months. (The titles and order are subject to change.)

What Is Man? By Robert Calhoun.
Right and Wrong. By Gregory Vlastos.
Christians in an Unchristian Society. By Ernest Fremont Tittle.
Why Religion? By Dean Robert Wicks.
Christian Faith. By Henry P. Van Dusen.

The publication of these books is a coöperative, non-profit enterprise for everybody concerned.

E. A. Yarrow,
For the Edward W. Hazen Foundation.

TO MY DAUGHTER
SARAH MALCOLM STEWART

CONTENTS

BISHOP. Now! Tell me about your church.

MANSON. I am afraid you may not consider it an altogether substantial concern. It has to be seen in a certain way, under certain conditions. Some people never see it at all. You must understand, this is no dead pile of stones and unmeaning timber. *It is a living thing.*

BISHOP. Numberless millions!

MANSON. When you enter it you hear a sound—a sound as if some mighty poem chanted. Listen long enough, and you will learn that it is made up of the beating of human hearts, of the nameless music of men's souls—that is, if you have ears. If you have eyes, you will presently see the church itself—a looming mystery of many shapes and shadows, leaping sheer from floor to dome. The work of no ordinary builder!

BISHOP. On the security of one man's name!

MANSON. The pillars of it go up like the brawny trunks of heroes: the sweet human flesh of men and women is moulded about its bulwarks, strong, impregnable: the faces of little children laugh out from every corner-stone: the terrible spans and arches of it are the joined hands of comrades; and up in the heights and spaces there are inscribed the numberless musings of all the dreamers of the world. It is yet building— building and built upon. Sometimes the work goes forward in deep darkness: sometimes in blinding light: now beneath the burden of unmutterable anguish: now to the tune of a great laughter and heroic shoutings like the cry of thunder. Sometimes, in the silence of the night-time, one may hear the tiny hammerings of the comrades at work up in the dome—the comrades that have climbed ahead.

Charles Rann Kennedy, in *The Servant in the House.*

CHAPTER I

THE TRAGIC FATE OF MAN IN THE MODERN WORLD

In order to appraise the Church's value and contribution to men and society, it is necessary to know the spiritual setting in which men find themselves, the nature of the Church, and the Church's response to the human scene.

A. THE WORLD WAR AS A MAJOR SPIRITUAL CATASTROPHE

In the years that followed the war beginning in 1914, and the consequent revolutions and counter-revolutions, society descended into a chaos that burned up the fruits of a century of culture and of industry. Obvious losses were the eleven million killed, the widows and orphans, the destruction of material, buildings, land, and transport. These brought in their train a destruction of trade and of culture. The death of young and talented men desperately needed today as leaders, censorship of the press, suppression of free speech, and the building of enthusiasms by hatred have clouded thought and confused purposes.

In addition, many of the old religious landmarks in the nature of both persons and doctrines were swept away. In Europe, when Nicholas I as head of the State and Church in Russia, Wilhelm II as the head of the established church in Germany, and Franz-Josef (who held a

1

special guardianship over the Roman Catholic Church in Austria-Hungary), no longer reigned, a vacuum was left in the thought of their people. Established churches were disestablished. The position of religious teachers declined. The clergy were no longer accorded the privileges and dignities that they had formerly received as public officials. The confusion of religion and patriotism that occurred in every nation was soon revealed to be a major intellectual and spiritual catastrophe. Thoughtful men everywhere lost faith in leadership that called upon the Prince of Peace to bless the methods of modern warfare. Enormous numbers untimely killed raised the ancient question: "If a man dies, shall he live again?" The problem of evil afflicted mankind. In the Old World, shattered churches, discredited because they had been too closely connected with fallen governments, were unable to give clear, spiritual assurance to suffering peoples. Harsh treaties and the breaking of their pledged word by men and nations brought a political and ethical relativism that was quickly communicated to the moral life of whole peoples. Men did not know, and they do not know, where to turn for honor, integrity and direction. In the New World, churchmen were puzzled by a growing indifference and by sharp questions that they were unable to answer.

The peace treaties remade the map of Europe, and thereby created a minorities problem involving spiritual questions of the first magnitude. Before the war there were four thousand kilometers of frontier in Europe; now there are ten thousand. Astride these frontiers, in zones from one to fifty kilometers wide, are some ten million minority peoples cut off from their parent, linguistic, political, and church groups. In hardly a new nation do these minority peoples enjoy the liberties they were promised. From this area of misery, sown with post-war hatred, has arisen a lush crop of cynicism and bitterness.

The church institutions of the Old World suffered severe shocks. The geographical rearrangement of the map brought with it division and impoverishment. In not a few nations, much of the material equipment of the churches was either badly damaged or destroyed. War killed much of their future leadership, inflation wiped out their endowments, disease weighed heavily upon them. In the hour of the people's greatest need, many churches were able to make only a feeble response. Dismembered and truncated bodies cannot function as healthy organisms.

The war in and of itself was a major spiritual shock— the objectivization of the greed, pride, and bloodthirstiness that were its antecedents. The Four Horsemen of the Apocalypse made clear a teaching that governments neglected: in modern life when one nation suffers, all suffer.

B. THE CENTRIFUGAL FORCES RELEASED IN THE MODERN WORLD

Before the Great War, with the exception of a few localities, boundaries were fairly stable. Some shifts had taken place after the Balkan Wars, and some rearrangements were made from time to time in Asia and Africa. There were territories that nations demanded as a right or that they had lost and wanted to reclaim. These situations created tensions but no one thought these tensions would cause war. People were held together, if only by the power of heavy-handed governments. With a disastrous peace following a ruinous war, divisive and centrifugal forces were released which not only split peoples apart but left confusion and division within the individual.

These centrifugal forces were manifested among the peoples of the world by the quick rise of a militant nationalism. Fear, hatred, localism, and irrationalism—factors always latent in society—came to the fore. In addition to these tensions, mankind faced the sheer intellectual incapacity to handle its problems. Herd instinct forced terrified peoples together for mutual protection within familiar localities. This process brought with it a growing fear of other groups or states. The world of politics, of economics, and of religion went through a period of confusion and dismemberment. Back-breaking armament and every form of restriction to trade impoverished governments and strangled commerce. In their effort to protect themselves and in their fear of neighbor nations, peoples let their national life ebb away behind protective tariff walls.

The forces of division also showed themselves within every state. Extreme party divisiveness occurred everywhere. In several lands parties began to build up private uniformed forces. Nationalism destroyed true patriotism. It became a collectivism that made cool, moral judgment upon men and events impossible. "My country, right or wrong," became the rallying cry. Striking posters appeared in many countries: "German folk, buy German wares"; "Buy British"; "Buy French"; "Buy American." The leaders of states began to create a theology and to organize a conscience for the people based upon mythologies dealing with soil, race, or national destiny. They set up principles of education based upon unsound historical conclusions. Several governments assumed that they were not only the best possible organization for society, but also exercised no little missionary spirit in exporting their ideas to other lands. We saw the rise not only of neo-paganism, but also of new secular religions, such as communism, nationalism, racialism, and fascism. These new human collectives have many of the attributes of the older religions: membership, rituals, social programs, discipline, and (most important and sinister) their own absolutes, which take the place of God and function as the final arbiter between ideas and men. The spirit of man had no protection from its own government. The Italian slogan, "Obey, believe, fight," typical of the attitude of many nations, reduced the status of man's mind to that of the barracks, the drill ground, or the prison.

The ultimate result of these centrifugal forces was to breed hatred, fear, and localism, to disrupt society, and to confuse the minds of individuals. This process finally led, because of man's desire not only to relieve himself of responsibility but to achieve some adequate way of life, into a radical reintegration of life in authoritarian or totalitarian states with a man or a party completely dominating politics, press, education, and industry. At the present time this urge for complete triumph of a new and regimented body of thought is laying heavy hands upon the Church, which contains within itself the last remnants of freedom in not a few countries. But whereas strong men, backed by obedient parties, were reintegrating the chaotic fragments that broke down under the centrifugal forces released by war, they have been unable to unify the souls of men. For the average man in Essen, Warsaw, Kiev, Lyons, Manchester, or Omaha something very profound has occurred; his loyalties are shaken, he can still obey or even fight—he can no longer easily believe.

C. THE SECULARIZATION OF LIFE

It is an obvious fact that many of the institutions founded by and for centuries conducted by the Church have now slipped into secular hands. This is true to a notable extent of schools, colleges, and hospitals. We cannot object to men of good will taking over these institutions and carrying them on. But the Church, as it did during the Middle Ages, faces the difficult problem of how to spiritualize a larger section of life. This is not a problem for the clergy alone. There are thousands of honest laymen who wonder how they can put Christian ideals into practice in their business and professional life, and many of them are making noble efforts in this direction. They find, however, that the spiritualization of business is against the grain of modern life.[1]

The deeper problem lies in the fact that surrounded by a society whose trends are all in a secular direction,

---

[1] For a full discussion of the problems connected with the application of Christian ideals to everyday life, and especially to business conduct, see Tead, Ordway, *The Case for Democracy*, Association Press, 1938 ($1.25).

the Church itself, *to a large degree,* has become secular. It must first save its own soul before it can save the soul of society. Education, commercialized amusements, improved modes of transportation, the exciting new world of the cinema, and the pressure of commercialism, have created a state of mind within society that does not make a fertile seed bed for faith. The Church has been colored by the life about it.

D. THE DEHUMANIZATION OF MAN

To some extent this process has been going on ever since the industrial revolution. At no time has man encountered that measure of justice, tolerance, and mutual aid from his fellow men that enabled man to attain his true stature. The moral confusion that brought about the war, the destruction of leadership, the consequent suffering, and the despair that has led to the present totalitarian states has so discouraged and beaten down the spirit of men that millions have thrown over individual judgment and voluntarily given themselves over to collectives of various kinds. There is no hope for men as long as they voluntarily dehumanize themselves. So widespread is this phenomenon that no one person can be blamed exclusively. Neither Stalin, Mussolini, nor Hitler were creators of this state of mind—they capitalized what they found. Neither they nor the people they lead were completely aware of the subconscious, subterranean processes within society that have made this voluntary handing over of individual liberty an almost universal characteristic of our times. Back of this mass drift toward collectives of Right and Left stand the shadowy figures of Nietzsche and Marx, whose systems of thought are battling for the mastery of the earth.

This blind allegiance to man or party, this impulse to give oneself to a collective is not decreasing. The herd instinct, augmented to the point of hysteria by fear, spiritual loneliness, hatred, and the intellectual incapacity to find solutions for their problems, drives men to these new faiths. The dictatorships and centralized governments of today are caused largely by man's own devaluation of himself. He yields himself unconditionally to authority.

Man has to worship something; and he has substituted political leaders, parties, and economic and social theory for God. He worships himself as he cheers the person he sets up to exercise the sovereign human functions he should have kept. Thus, thinking himself God, he has reduced and divided his own humanity.

It is because the Church stands for the dignity of individual men as sons of God that any attempt to take from him his freedom of choice and his critical powers finds the Church in irrevocable opposition to all totalitarian theories of state. This stand has brought upon the Church persecution unknown since the Middle Ages.

E. The Continuing Economic Crisis

Millions of our fellow citizens, and millions more people throughout the world, are workless and poor on a planet that has the possibility of food, shelter, clothing, schools, hospitalization, and happiness for all. Under nearly every plan for relief, men, women, and children are disintegrating morally as well as suffering physically.

Neither private philanthropy nor public aid can be accepted as a permanent solution for large numbers who would gladly work if they could find work. Although nearly all agree that the happiest solution would be private employment for all at an adequate wage, nevertheless, when private employment and philanthropy break down, manifest injustice is done if government does not step in to assist. Restrictions to commerce, underhousing, malnutrition, and the spiritual effects of idleness are having a profoundly demoralizing effect, whereas the hope of employment by men and women approaching the lowering age limit is further discouraged by the advance of invention. With the filling up of unoccupied lands, with actual and threatened war, with the monetary and industrial situation unstable, few men are so sanguine as to hope that the continuing economic crisis will be quickly healed.

Economic ills that afflict many nations in various forms and intensities are due not only to weaknesses in fascism and communism but in capitalism as well. The Church's function is not to oppose one type of social and economic set-up to another, but to labor for justice for every individual and group whatever be the contemporary arrangement. Obviously, fascism, communism, and capitalism are all inimical to the best forms of religion unless checked and disciplined by Christian teachings and a Christian conscience.

F. The Search for Solutions

Men, confused and almost stupefied by problems that seem insurmountable, are turning with questions to every institution. They find governments unable to give them what they need, to increase their spiritual prospects as men. They find the press incapable to guide them; they discover industry caught in its own technical troubles or in the toils of government regulation. Education has failed to produce that race of philosophers that Plato hoped could form enlightened governors. Go where they will, men find few to answer the questions that frame their fears.

What then of the Church? The Church must be courageous enough to confess that it has been too much wedded to contemporary culture. In many states it has confused national aims with spiritual purposes. In some instances it has lost itself in social enthusiasms that are not different from the secular efforts of the day. In others it has given itself to saving individual souls without reference to an environment that breaks the spirits and the bodies of men. It must confess to denominational bias and doctrinal prejudices that have rent that unity which is a dominant feature of the Church as a universal fellowship. It must confess to having identified matters of taste with fundamental matters of faith. It must admit having been so enamored of some particular type of theology that at times it has refused to allow for the continuing impact of the Spirit of God to bring further light to the minds of men. The first thing the Church must do is to confess its own sin.

But the Church has not been altogether false or weak in attempting to face the situation in which modern man finds himself. Have we asked the Church to make solutions that men should make for themselves? Should the

Church be called upon to halt the iron sequence of cause and effect? Should a parent always intervene to save a child from the consequence of his own foolish acts? Or have we asked the Church for the wrong things? The Church and the state are both, according to New Testament religion, ordained of God. There is a secular order and there is a spiritual order. (This does not mean, however, that any form of government represents the will of God or that the best governments the world has seen could not have been vastly improved by the free play of Christian ethics upon its acts and officials.) Have we demanded that the Church produce those benefits that a state wisely and ethically run should bring to pass? Or have we seen a few unfaithful in the Church and made a false generalization that all are so? Have we been able to discriminate between those things wherein the Church is true and those in which it has been false to its ideals? Can we not see that, even if every man in the Church be false, the Church's Lord is still the one intellect, the one leader adequate to create character and provide guidance capable of handling the tensions of modern life?

Most men and women of the Western World have had some connection with the Church. It is hardly an exaggeration to say that a large section of these believe the Church has wholly or partly failed. Is their opinion based upon objective fact? Or, if it be admitted that the Church has not wholly failed, has it succeeded in enough areas to justify its existence and its claim to the loyalties of men?

At peril of its life the Church must remove from itself the reproach so common today that as an institution it has become irrelevant to the sharp difficulties of our day.

Has the Church lost its relevance to the human scene
through neglect, has it forgotten the adventure of faith,
the cleansing danger of truly faithful living? Has it lost
itself in discussion? Has it denied its own nature by refusing to see that, whether it will or not, it is an extension
of the life of Christ in the modern world? Pronouncements, solemnity, resolutions, conservatism, sporadic
radicalism, overheated crusades against this or that evil,
a fragmentary approach to life—none of these attitudes or
activities can suffice for the abiding faith, the sound sense,
and the overwhelming, sacrificial love and holy purpose
that the Church can and must derive from Jesus as its
leader. The Church is in a unique sense the keeper of
tremendous spiritual resources emanating from the life
and teachings of its Founder. It must exercise those resources as a spiritual trustee of our generation.

Reverently or bitterly, with genuine curiosity or with
almost savage doubt, not a few are asking what guidance
the Church may give in a period of confusion, hatred,
and ethical relativity. The lives of men are woven by
unbreakable threads into the fabric of state, industry,
education, community, church, and home. Does the
Church's past instruction and performance in regard to
these major interests offer any guarantee of present help?
What is the Church that claims so great wisdom? What
has it to offer in a day replete with danger on many fronts?

CHAPTER II

THE CHURCH'S PLACE IN THE MODERN WORLD

A. Two Major Conceptions of the Church

At the outset of any consideration of the visible Church it is well to point out that the main lines of difference are not along the lines of Roman Catholic, Protestant, and Eastern Orthodox, but rather in regard to two major conceptions of the Church's function. The first regards the Church as an inclusive agency of salvation, the second, as an exclusive community of saints.[1] The two concepts are generally designated the church type and the sect type. Catholics have taken both views at different periods. They have preserved the value of the sect type in the monastic orders. By "sect" we mean here an exclusive type of church life best represented in America by denominations that do not allow members of other churches to partake of communion with them and who definitely feel that spiritual safety is to be gained only through their mode of life. As a matter of fact, if the Church is holy, it is usually not Catholic in the universal sense, and, if Catholic, it is usually not so rigorous in moral standards as the sect type. In actual practice there is a merging of the two ideas in several communions. Episcopalians and Presbyterians have attempted to embrace both emphases.

The Church as an inclusive agency of salvation is con-

[1] See Bainton, Roland H., in *Church History*, June, 1932, pp. 3-25.

cerned to reach as many as possible, and for that reason is willing to meet them on their own level, attempting to raise them in the scale of moral and spiritual values. The sect or community of saints is also concerned in making more saints, but especially in preserving the primitive patterns of faith and practice, even if membership be small.[2] It is true there is now a gradual blurring of these two opposing concepts, but the ideas have had great influence throughout history—and still have.

B. THE IDEAL AND THE ACTUAL CHURCH

In some instances Saint Paul speaks of the Church as if it were even then perfect, "without spot or blemish." However, as we read his letters, especially those to the Corinthians, we are aware of grave moral problems with which the early Church was afflicted. Its members lived in the world and were influenced by it, even as today. Saint Paul kept before his associates the ideal Church, but he never forgot the Church made up of men and women of flesh and bone represented by congregations at Jerusalem, Ephesus, Smyrna, Rome, Thessalonika, and elsewhere. Our hope today is not to revert to some pristine glory but rather to understand and be obedient to that same Spirit that was the source of all that was gay, enduring, and spiritually responsive in the early Church. Taking a historical view of the short span that twenty centuries make, the Church today is still primitive. We are still in the school-boy stage.

---

[2] See Troeltsch, Ernst, *Social Teachings of the Christian Churches*, 2 vols., Macmillan, New York, 1931 ($10.50), for an extended discussion of this point. See especially "Sect-Type and Church-Type Contrasted," pp. 331-343, vol. I.

We are, perhaps, not justified in expecting a perfect Church at some more or less definite future date. We know, however, that if the Church is ever to approximate perfection, it will have as its component parts all the beauty and all the insight and all the likeness to Christ that is our true inheritance from Jewish prophets, from Jesus, from the great interpretations in the New Testament, and from the experience of just men of every tribe and tongue. It will be enriched by both prophet and priest, by Eastern mystic, by simple piety, by the scholars' valor, by carefully conserved tradition, by Sacraments, and by the free impact of the Spirit upon the mind of man. If impoverished by no fear, halted by no prejudice against the experience of others, it will be amplified and deepened by the word and life of all spiritual men.

C. The Church's Unique Character

The modern man rightly asks what unique qualities the Church possesses that justify its claim to spiritual leadership.

It is well to keep clearly in mind different concepts behind the word "Church." The "Church Universal," the local church or parish, and the denomination have many common characteristics as well as certain differences.

"The Church Universal is essentially the extension of the life of Christ in the world and embraces all who are in union with Christ," to use a statement from the deliberations of the Commission on the Nature and Function of the Church in preparation for the meeting of the International Missionary Council at Madras, India, in 1938.

The Edinburgh Conference of Faith and Order of 1937 stated: "We agree that the Church is the Body of Christ and the blessed company of all faithful people, whether in heaven or on earth, the communion of saints." Again Edinburgh stated, "We are at one in confessing belief in the Holy Catholic Church. The Church is . . . the household of God, the family in which the fatherhood of God and the brotherhood of man is to be realized in the children of his adoption. It is the body of Christ, whose members derive their life and oneness from their one living Head." Here we are describing the universal, invisible Church, the *Una Sancta,* the one Holy, Catholic Church, embracing all believers in Christ of every age, in its unity amid diversity.

The local church is a local fellowship of all who profess and call themselves Christians. Some would include children or at least baptized children in this definition. Some would require that such a local congregation should be established by ecclesiastical authority. Few would deny the name Church to an orderly congregation of Christians because of the absence of strict ecclesiastical regularity. We know what is meant when we speak of the local Baptist or Congregational or Episcopal church.

A denomination is an organization of larger or smaller groups of local churches based on agreement in doctrine, polity, or service.

It must be admitted honestly that Christians do not and probably never will agree upon any one form of visible organization, be it local, regional, or world wide. Therefore, we must note two major concepts of the denomination:

First, "Several branches of Christendom believe that the only visible Church is the local organization of believers who recognize no ecclesiastical authority superior to themselves. This point of view is held by Baptists, Disciples, Congregationalists, and kindred Churches."

Second, "A second category of Churches hold that the visible Church is something more than the purely local expression found in the parish, that the Church may have a true visible expression in an organization of all who are making an attempt to give a concrete expression to the Universal Church. This category would include Episcopalian, Presbyterian, Lutheran, and other bodies of a kindred ecclesiastical outlook.

"Both types of regional, national, or international organization of local parishes, whether they consider themselves a Church, as such, a voluntary association of parishes, feel equally that they are divinely commissioned to be something more than a local organization of believers."[8]

Both would also agree that they are only a partial expression of the invisible Church Universal.

In what way, then, is the visible Church considered as a local fellowship, as a denomination, or as world-wide groupings of denominations or communions unique? The Church is different from all other groupings in several significant ways, whenever it is true to its own nature. That it often fails is admitted by any sincere churchman.

It Brings a Critique to All of Life

No other institution is in such a singular manner called upon to witness to truth, love, justice, and mercy as is the Church. Because of its nature it must make an ap-

---

[8] See The Minutes of The Commission on Nature and Function of the Church for the Madras Meeting of the International Missionary Council, especially the paper on "The Church Universal, The Local Church and The Denomination," by Professor Robert Hastings Nichols.

praisal and a judgment upon all human affairs and can never complain when the sharpest scrutiny is correspondingly directed toward all its works and ways.

All attempts to reunite a dissolving civilization around such concepts as race, soil, nation, or class, or any effort to secure the advantage of one segment of humanity to the detriment of others must be scrutinized by the Church and must receive its judgment. The Church is performing this difficult task better than many think, and in hard places. Witness the stand of many pastors in Germany against the dehumanization of man and the seizure of his liberties. The Church insists that the love of God and his beneficial purpose are basic realities that God not only revealed Himself in the person of Jesus Christ but also that Jesus in His life and teaching gave an example of what man might be; that in His crucifixion He showed not only the gravity of sin but the length to which love will go in forgiveness and in overcoming evil; that persons of every race are equally valuable before God; that men should love their neighbor as themselves; that they can unite in a fellowship in which they can fully realize themselves and discover all the meanings God has for them individually and socially. Because of such insistence, to be true to its own nature, the Church brings a critique to all of life.

It Must Courageously Look Forward to Suffering

The Church is also different in that it must courageously look forward to suffering, not to a success based upon a diminution of the teachings of Jesus to make them acceptable to the governments, to the taste, or the moral standards of the day. Wherever national pride or military power is unbridled, there true Christians are meeting their test, and there, inevitably, the Church is singled out as an enemy of the national ideal; for its allegiance is above that of any state. It faces and will face persecution on two grounds.

In the first place, the Church is not a local affair. The member of the First Baptist Church of Keokuk or of an Anglican Chapel in a London slum is not first of all a member of the American, Iowan, Baptist Christian community, or of the Established, Anglican persuasion. He is a member of the Christian Church that is part of a universal community, and is so recognized by governments and men even when they taunt the Church for its divisions. Thus the very nature of the Church as an ecumenical, universal community transcending tongue, tribe, nation, and color is always in danger of arousing adherents of localism, racialism, and nationalism or any partisan body that threatens the freedom of the human spirit. The Church is not unpatriotic. No organization has done more to foster true love of village, city, or nation. It has asserted and is asserting now, in peril of its life in many lands, that rampant nationalism is patriotism corrupted by pride, greed, or the lust of power.

In the second place, the Church has suffered and will inevitably suffer because it must state without compromise that its members and the Church as an organic whole must give supreme obedience to God. It has a prior allegiance above self, family, state, race, culture, or nation. Secular governments have always looked askance at any divided allegiance.

The Church Is Always Dying and Rising Again

In this it shares the experience of its founder. At any one period, judged by its own best ethical standards, the Church fails. Massacres, persecutions, popular indifference, priestly corruption have at many periods all but destroyed faith among sections of mankind, but through some power of resuscitation the Church has sprung into life again. After tribulation the Church comes back purified and enriched by the experience. Paradoxically, it is never strongest in a true spiritual sense when it achieves an easy *rapprochement* with contemporary culture. It is strongest when pressing hard its ethical claims upon men and society. Yet it must never take perverse pleasure in unpopularity or in the smallness of its numbers, never lose sight of its goal—the extension of loyalty to Christ in word and deed as far as the habitation of men.

It Is Conscious at the Same Moment of Being Saved and Lost

It is at the same moment a congregation of sinners and of saints. It feels a solid satisfaction in the spirit and heroism of its Leader, and in the life and teaching of its most spiritual souls. Nevertheless, it knows that this satisfaction can never become pride without defeating itself—that all its gifts are held in stained hands—that it must work out its salvation with fear and trembling—that virtue cannot be stored up, but must be used to be kept. Whenever the Church has become popular and powerful, whenever it has had too much control of lands, politics, and education, it has fallen a prey to pride. Often when it has seemed weakest it has been strongest, developing its great thinkers and saints under pressure of hardship.

It Is the Chief Mediator of God to Men

The Church, as a matter of historical fact, has been the major channel through which the revelation of God in Jesus Christ is given to men. By this is meant more than ritual, history, tradition, and artistic media such as painting, music, architecture, glass, and all other forms that have been used to express the Christian message. The Church is more than all the means it employs. It is a living organism built essentially of personal relationships, unique in that they are derived from and directed toward faith in a personal God. The Church is, therefore, the carrier of Christian truth to every new generation. It is only when a man enters into this fellowship, shares its knowledge, its ideals, its hopes, its central faith in God that he enters into his full inheritance of Christian love, work, and belief. Then the Church becomes for him the body of Christ, of which he is a member, and through it he discovers the will of God and his own true value and destiny. Man discovered his place in a fabric of such values as honesty, purity, and love; a realm of ideals that he helps to realize, a realm Jesus called the Kingdom of God.

It Has a Unique Pastoral Relationship

The Church is also unique in that it has a pastoral relation to men, women, and children possessed by no other human organization. It recognizes that men as men are the children of God and as such are to be respected and befriended. No other institution has been given so high a conception of compassion and friendliness, of neighborly service and redemptive love. Jesus lifted personality to a new dignity and value. The Church must always incarnate the figure of the Good Shepherd. Outside Christianity there is no servant of the people comparable to the Christian pastor.

It Is Concerned With the Whole of Life

The Church is also unique in having a concern for the whole of life. There are many organizations that care for the body or mind of particular age groups, but none outside the Church that seek to relate themselves to the body, mind, and spirit of both sexes throughout life in every personal and social relationship. Because of this inclusive concern the Church often senses fresh needs in the community before they are recognized by other institutions. In this function it has many times created institutions to meet newly discovered needs that it has later surrendered or turned over to other auspices. Witness schools, colleges, hospitals, social service agencies, child guidance, and family welfare units, which the Church has initiated and which are now run by men and women of good will, but not under definite Church auspices.

Because the Church is the champion of the value of man as a child of God, it is urged, especially by those of prophetic mind, to battle for many reforms. Parties, denominations, and combinations of denominations have often done so, sometimes with effectiveness, accomplishing solid results for human betterment. Sometimes churches have exhausted their energies on matters of passing interest. The Church's aid is sought constantly by groups of every point of view. Obviously, it cannot serve every cause. Its membership embraces men of different points of view regarding the best way to deal with war, unemployment, and industrial relationships. Its purpose is best served by being neither essentially an organization for social reform, nor as an auxiliary of any economic school or political party. It does its best work in helping men achieve their true nature in union with God, and as free agents to work out their destiny in obedience to Him throughout the whole series of social and economic textures into which our lives are interwoven.

The Church has a group experience extending over many generations. In a sense it has a group memory that cautions it against detailed blueprints of Utopia, of which there are many in every decade, especially in times of crisis. It should keep the light of the spirit burning bright, sending its sons and daughters to combat injustice and to establish order, goodness, and happiness. To it they may come for inspiration, to it retire for the healing of their wounds. Sometimes the Church must be a solace; at other times a goad. Discoverers, prophetic geniuses, seers, dreamers of a better social order are always fewer than the conservers. Within the membership of the Church, fiery souls should find aids for their vision, strength for their battle, and patience to understand that their dream would be impossible of attainment if everyone dreamed with equal intensity.

Radical thought is very often the divine ferment that energizes those who are tempted to overconservatism, whereas the values of radicalism are often saved by the inertia of conservatives, even though the slowing-up process may be painful to eager spirits who want the Kingdom of God to come immediately.

The point to be kept in mind here is that there must be not only liberty, but outgoing hospitality, toward all types who are seeking to find the will of God for the constantly changing human scene. Only in a truly liberal and generous atmosphere will it be possible to have the best thought and action of the many types embraced within its membership.

Neither radical nor conservative sections can ethically employ methods or coercion to secure a false appearance of unanimity. Because of its fundamental respect for individual conscience the Church may easily seem laggard in the whole matter of social reform, an accusation that has often proved true on lesser grounds.

It Is the Only Universal Fellowship

The Church brings a conception of brotherhood not only to the individual on Main Street or in Mayfair, but seeks to have all men and women recognize their unity as the children of God. No other conception of brotherhood embraces all lesser unities. The Church opposes a centripetal force, love of men as God's sons, to centrifugal forces that tend to disrupt the individual and to shatter the unity of mankind. The Church is thus unique in being, whether its members and clergy in any one place or time recognize it or not, a universal fellowship. The Church can never have barriers or limits that quite naturally form the frontiers of so many organizations within society. Its object is a community as broad as mankind.

It is not only world-wide in extent, it is also continuous in time. Our fathers' fathers united with the Church even as we have joined it. Space does not break its unity, nor death disrupt its fellowship. For a Church based upon Jesus' resurrection, the grave does not divide the living from the dead. According to the Christian faith we all live and shall live in Him.

The completed Church will possess the ethical characteristics of the Westerner at his best, the mystical insight of the Indian, the determination of many Japanese believers to bring the kingdom of God now in practical measures, the elasticity of the Korean, the liturgical genius of the Russian, the passionate enthusiasm of the African, the inner light of the Quaker, the subtlety of the Spaniard, the decorum of churches with an historic episcopate, and the less formal services of the freer churches. High Church, Low Church, Free Church, Roman Church, Eastern Church—all have rare gifts. We impoverish ourselves when we refuse to appreciate them. Our home towns will never be fully Christian until Chicago, Madras, and Rio are in allegiance to Christ. The Church will never have the complete resources that are in Christ until society also has become loyal to Him.

It Combines Both the Human and the Divine Element

The Church has all the weakness of the human material composing its membership. It also draws a perennial power of resuscitation from its source in the love and will of God which were concretely set forth in history in the person and work of Jesus Christ. Thus the Church is unique in its essential character, being supra-natural in that it is of God and for God, divine, eternal, and holy. And this is true whether one views the Church as existing only in individual parishes or as great regional, national, or world-wide combinations. The fellowship within the Church is different from all other associations, for in it the believer is living within a series of relationships that are in process of being cleansed and purified by the redeeming work of Christ. Actually, those relationships often fall short of the ideal—but more than in any other association men are haunted and often tortured by this ideal, and are led to progressive approximation of it. The human and the divine factors are both at work.

It Is the Extension of the Life of Christ into the Life of Today

The local fellowship or a denomination, at its best, no less than the invisible, Universal Church should be an extension of the life of Christ.

It is the Body of which He is the Head. God gave to men in Jesus the fullness of His life and inasmuch as the Church derives its existence, nature, purpose, and guidance from Him, the Church must in word, deed, and spirit be sharply aware of both its resources and its responsibility.

The Church is unique among the communities of men because it brings a critique to all of life, looks forward courageously to suffering, is always dying and rising again, is conscious at the same moment of being saved and lost, is the chief mediator of God to men, has a unique pastoral relationship, is concerned with the whole of life, is the only universal fellowship, combines both the human and the divine element, and is an extension of the life of Christ into the chaotic present.

CHAPTER III

THE AUTHORITY OF THE CHURCH

A. Various Views of Authority

Some may ask, why be interested in authority in the Church? Shouldn't religion be a matter of persuasion only? In a sense this is true. Nevertheless, order is the first rule of life. We must employ organization to communicate faith, religious experience, and the teachings of Jesus from one generation to another. There must be some point of reference and some standard for judgment. To prevent chaos the Church must have certain rules of order, discipline, and procedure. Out of need, authority arises. No team can play well for long without a coach or a rule book. No intricate body of thought, no vast web of human relationships such as constitute the Church could long function effectively without some form of government and the power to enforce its rules. Men must have some recognized body of experience by which they can test their faith.

A distinction, of course, must be made between authority that has to do with the truth or authenticity of the Church's teaching, and authority in the government, regulations, and administration of Church affairs. Authority is needed in the first instance to keep teaching pure amid the shifting scenes, languages, and modes of thought of the ongoing generations. This authority, which has to do with the Church's witness to the truth, derives from God's revelation of Himself in historic instances, as in Jesus and through his Spirit operating in the life and thought of men in any age.

Authority is needed in the second instance—that is, in government—in order that the fellowship of Jesus' followers may handle their common problems effectively and provide a system of worship, instruction, and discipline most helpful to the individual. Without some authority the Church as an organized device for the better expression of faith and its works would fall into chaos.

The Church has various views of authority. We often hear "the religion of the spirit" contrasted with "the religion of authority." In some quarters, indeed, the religion of the spirit is apt to mean following any enthusiasm, no matter if it leads us from the main lines of New Testament and Church experience into vague and esoteric practice. Authority is shunned as something despotic. Nevertheless, order is one of the major rules of life, in the spiritual as in the material world.

In the early Church the influence of the Holy Spirit did not result in revolt against authority. By "Holy Spirit" we mean that outreaching of God not dissimilar to the outreach of any personality to persuade or to rebuke others. God's spirit was then, and is now, the fountainhead of authority. The Spirit is a testimony to the truth, not a goad that drives unwilling souls into a uniformity in which there is no true unity.

It has been a Protestant characteristic, especially among the smaller evangelical sects, to object to authority in the Church. While denying the infallibility of the Church, they often proclaim the infallibility of the Bible or some verse or chapter of the Bible; or of some Confession or Creed. Martin Luther stated the matter far better when he said that authority was not to be found in the letter of the Bible but in the Spirit of God speaking through the pages of the Bible and understood by spiritual man. This view of Luther's is far more acceptable to modern men who find difficulty with claims for either a perfect Book or a perfect Church. The only perfection lies in God, revealed in the flesh in Jesus Christ, and continually communicated in love and power to men through the working of His Spirit.

B. The Meaning of Authority

Authority in the Church is based upon or assumes some revelation of God. By "revelation" we mean that process by which the nature of God is made plain, not only to the five senses but also to those subtle factors of the intellect by which men lay hold upon realities that are invisible and intangible.

Authority in one view could be said to have a basis of pessimism provided we hold that the faith had once and forever been revealed, that God does not continually speak, or that our time is lacking in sensitive souls.

A more optimistic view is held by those who believe God still leads men into further truth as they are capable of receiving it. No Church could long exist without an underlying basis of revelation; that is, we must have some background upon which to build a system of thought or an organization of believers. One need not take the extreme position, however, that the faith has once and for all been completely delivered. Of course, interpretation and teaching are a primary obligation upon the Church before it has a right to ask for obedience. Nevertheless, authority—that authority which is before men in past revelation, such as exists in the teaching and mind of Jesus—is to be obeyed.

In the Roman Catholic church, where the government is more closely knit, severe penalties are imposed for disobedience to authority. In Protestant communions, the rules are less strict.

Fundamentally, authority cannot be considered in the abstract; it is based upon a personal response rooted in loyalty, reverence, or admiration for a person or institution. The Catholic emphasizes the authority of the Church; the sect type of Protestant generally emphasizes the absolute authority of the Bible.

Authority may mean either *auctoritas,* a commanding influence, or *potestas,* dogmatic prescriptive power. Authority in the Church as far as it relates to witnessing to the truth is *auctoritas*. It should mean nothing despotic; rather, it should mean something reasonable and helpful—namely, respect for responsible statements and requirements laid down by accredited representatives of the Church whose experience and knowledge have given them a position akin to that of authorities in any other field. There are numerous instances in every field of life and work when one's own experience is too slight to furnish a basis for sound action. There is a corporate witness of trained and experienced people in economics, politics, education, science, and art. There is also a corporate witness of competent opinion in religion. Authority has often been used to prevent experiment, but this abuse should not blind our eyes to its true function.

One need not accept any body of teaching such as a creed without critical examination. This would be an exercise of authority as *potestas*. But it does help to accept the full inheritance of the Church, at least tentatively, in lieu of full faith. A mariner may rightly accept a compass he may suspect is imperfect. It serves to guide, until checking by horizon, star, sun, headland, and charts proves the truth or variation of his present instrument.

C. THE SOURCE OF THE CHURCH'S AUTHORITY

The Church comes with the authority of the religious experience of believers whose lives have been touched by the historical revelation of God in Jesus Christ. The Church is made of men of flesh and bone, with faulty intellects, but the statements of their experience can help. If a man thinks it not beneath him to be a humble student before a master painter or an engineering expert, can he think it beneath him to listen to Thomas Aquinas, Luther, Calvin, Father Damien, or Kagawa? It is not meant that these men are equal to Jesus, but that in every age God has not left himself without witness even though revelation has been an interrupted rather than a continuous process. These spirit-filled witnesses are able to instruct.

Although tradition often serves as a basis for those who would taunt the believer with the charge of "slave mentality," it has its proper place in religion as in any other interest in life. One cannot safely rely on contemporary thought alone. Devout and inspired men often disagree at any one period. Then one is helped by an appeal to the main historic tradition. Every great pursuit or noble inquiry has its tradition—the distilled wisdom of years of effort and contemplation—and to this body of experience the average man turns with gratitude. There is a racial or group experience—a group memory, if you will—a corporate achievement that is as valuable as the inspired work or words of any one man. We neglect the tested achievements and insights of the past at our peril. At one time we may do this through impatience, at another from ignorance, at still other moments from sheer pride. Meanwhile, those to whom life and God give capacity experiment further, constantly restating and clarifying the continuing life of the Spirit in the life of men and of the Church.

The Church has often been wrong in its action and in its pronouncements, but the sifted historical experience of a vast number of believers on a large number of problems is more apt to be right than individual conjectures upon a more limited experience. The freedom of individual thought and investigation must be preserved. It must be remembered, however, that although the Church's spiritual life depends upon the lighted minds of individual souls, nevertheless, light in the minds of individual souls most often comes from partaking of the illumination given through the years to the whole group. I may discover some ethical meaning for my town in Christ; you may find through prayer some resource that can encourage me; our neighbors linked to us in the Church may together work out the technique that can make our insight effective in social action. There is an accumulation of experience in any great field of human endeavor that the individual disregards at his peril. The Church's life and practice are built upon the accumulated experience of mankind as it attempts to gain union with God.

D. THE VALUE OF CREEDS AND CONFESSIONS

This is where Creeds and Confessions, used wisely and not as absolute yardsticks to measure men's souls, have an immense value. Some persons do not need them; some resist them. Nevertheless, it is reasonable to admit their value to many as a formative influence to give order to speculations upon the nature of God, man, nature, and the universe. Most men need relatively fixed points by which to steer; mariners of a different cast of mind can well appreciate this while they employ a different method.

Authority in the Church should not be a police officer to force others to believe our way. Authority is a witness to the truth that has been discovered as well as revealed in the spiritual experience of men in this and in all ages.

E. THE ORIGIN OF THE MINISTRY[1]

Again, one may ask, as with the question of authority, why be interested? If the values represented in Christ's teachings are worthy of preservation and continual interpretation to each oncoming generation, if those teachings tend toward group fellowship, it is inevitable that such a community will sooner or later select certain of its members to be specially charged with certain tasks. Two

---

[1] An excellent discussion of this matter occurs in Quick, Oliver Chase, *The Christian Sacraments*, London, 1927, pp. 123-160.

dangers are obviously inherent in the formation of a class of such men. The first is that they assume a proprietary right in their calling, arrogating to themselves powers that can be easily abused. The second danger is that the members turn over to a priestly class the duties and obligations that should be carried forward by all members of the group. Social psychology and the desire for practical effectiveness made the fellowship of the Christian Church inevitable. Once the group was formed, these factors operated in the selection of men with special qualifications for special tasks.

What was the nature of the Church's ministry? Any such group as the early Church, deeply stirred with a sense of mission to make their faith universal, would turn to practical ways of embodying and making effective their way of life. Being in the nature of a large family, they practised for a time a form of Christian communism. As the original group scattered, as other bands of believers were formed from the radiating center in Palestine, this form was given up, probably because of the diversity of callings and places of work. Holy Orders, the practice of formally designating and consecrating men whose special function was to serve and shepherd the spiritual life of the congregation, grew up as a practical necessity.[2]

Jesus left no legislation regarding the exact forms of the institution of the Church. There was a pre-institutional period when the Church was fired with prophetic zeal unchanneled in regular forms. That organization

---

[2] For detailed accounts of early Church organization, see Hatch, Edwin, *The Organization of the Early Christian Churches*, Longmans, New York, 1909 ($3.00); and Lowrie, Walter, *The Church and Its Organization*, London, 1904.

would come was inevitable, and, in fact, desirable; for organization, although it may be abused in any field, must precede the orderly employment of any force.

Many controversies have raged over Jesus' teaching about Holy Orders. He left no directions or legislation about the Church. Jesus laid down fundamental spiritual principles, but had faith enough in men to carry on his work using forms and methods derived from those principles that most appropriately met the need. His wisdom was nowhere more profound than in his practice of not legislating in detail regarding the life and practice of his followers who were soon to confront economic, political, and cultural situations, as the new faith spread, which were not identical with the conditions in Palestine.

From the outset the Church, or the community of the "called out," as a fully self-conscious group of Jesus' followers, had in its various centers men to whom was committed the conduct of public worship and the administration of the Sacraments, such as Baptism and the Holy Communion.

From New Testament accounts and elsewhere we learn that bishops, presbyters, and deacons were very early assigned to serve each group wherever the Lord's Supper was celebrated. These men probably received their authority from the original group who went out preaching and founding other Churches as Evangelists, Prophets, and Apostles. There were probably many situations where two or more bishops exercised their functions jointly. Some authorities hold that in isolated communities it is probable that such leaders were appointed by independent action of the congregation. In the beginning there were variations of procedure, of position, and of power, and many experiments. Similar instances have occurred along frontiers of civilization in every age, the whole process becoming more orderly as the population became stabilized.[3]

F. The Concept of the Gospel—a Determining Factor

The work of the ministry is largely conditioned by the underlying conceptions of what the Gospel is. For the Protestant mind, the Gospel, as manifested in the total Christian revelation, in the teaching of the New Testament, in the experience of godly men and women in the Church, in the glad news of salvation and forgiveness that Jesus communicated to the Apostles and they to the Church, is the main factor. The spoken word of the preacher, the personal persuasion of the unbeliever by the believer, is placed in the forefront of the Church's teaching. Baptism and the Lord's Supper are kept as covenant rites to seal a relationship to God, as well as a means of grace through which the Spirit communicates some special gift. It is by hearing and accepting the Gospel in faith that men are saved and are brought to the right relationship to God. Some groups, such as the Quakers, have no Sacrament at all. When General William Booth founded the Salvation Army he found so much controversy among scholars over the Sacraments,

---

[3] The *Didache* is an example of a short manual of Church administration in a day when bishops were highly esteemed. But even in this period the prophet or inspired preacher held the chief place. See *The Apostolic Fathers*, with an English translation by Kirsopp Lake, vol. I, Putnam, New York, 1930, pp. 303-333 ($2.50).

which he felt the average man could neither understand nor value, that he renounced them all in an effort to put the whole force of his valiant movement behind that preaching of the Gospel and in Christian service to under-privileged people.

Wide groups who conceive the Gospel as applied to politics, industry, education, and art obviously would expect activities, studies, and pronouncements upon the part of their clergy that would not be required of clergy serving groups who conceived the Gospel as applying only in a very personal relation between the individual and his God.

G. Priest or Prophet?

Regardless of how the ministry of the Church came into being, what is its nature today? Are these men, our servants in the Church, ordained by God or by men? They are in a true sense, if they be true men, ordained by both heaven and earth. A true minister feels that he has been called of God to his work. There is a wide variation among Protestant sects both in education and in ordina-tion. Certainly a better trained and more devoted min-istry is always one of the Church's greatest needs. Are these clergymen to be priests or prophets, or shall they attempt the difficult task of combining the characteristics of both?

Two powerful tendencies run through Hinduism, Mo-hamedanism, Christianity, and other spiritual move-ments. The first is conservative, bringing organization, creeds, rules, disciplines, confessions. Its purpose is to conceive and to safeguard the faith, and is represented by the priest. The second movement is radical, questioning incomplete statements, rigid views, exclusive practices, revolting against stuffiness, self-righteousness, and dogmatism. Its purpose is to rebuke, to stir up the life of the group, to place the vision of a better life before men. These fiery fouls sometimes stay in the community to quicken its spiritual tempo, sometimes they organize opposing sects, and at other times they go out as lone workers for a truer ideal. This movement is represented by the prophet.

Here also the two views of the Church have a determining influence. Those who view the Church as an inclusive agency of salvation are more apt to view their clergy in terms of priesthood. Those who conceive the Church as an exclusive community of saints look upon their clergy more as prophets. By "prophet" is generally meant a man called of God to preach. By "priest" we mean someone set aside by the Church, through regularly constituted exercises and studies, to be its servant. Ministers are generally regarded as prophets among Protestant church people. Catholics view their clergy as men consecrated to administer the Sacraments. Of course these two points of view are not mutually exclusive. The Protestant minister who is apt to rely on preaching and to minimize liturgy, taking to himself a great measure of independence, may at the same time rely heavily upon the administration of the Sacraments; and the Catholic priest may be an outstanding preacher of social righteousness. Of course, the priestly and the prophetic function may both have full play in the individual clergyman's life. Temperament and the denomination in which the clergyman serves do, however, have a powerful influence in determining whether a clergyman is chiefly a priest or a prophet.

Christendom can ill afford to deny the presence of God's Spirit an inspiration even in uncouth men without training who have preached the Gospel in power. It can also ill afford to allow the Church to fall into disorder by refusing to follow sound procedure, winnowed through years of experience.

CHAPTER IV

THE CHURCH'S TASK

When we say the Church ought to do this or that we are faced squarely with the problem of the nature of the Church. Is it an inclusive agency of salvation, an ark in which all men may claim a place, a spiritual home to which all are invited? Or is it an exclusive community of saints into which only those who have passed rigid examinations and who maintain a holy life are members? Great groups of individual parishes, such as the Episcopalians, call their total body a Church and would deny that they are a denomination. Large groups of Presbyterians and Methodists would use both denomination and Church to define their national or world organizations. Baptists, however, would maintain that only a local parish can be a Church—that the organization of all their parishes would constitute a denomination but not a Church. Of course there is a real sense in which the Church Universal embraces every Christian. Those who hold that only a local parish can be a Church would question whether even a local parish can collectively confess its blindness and sin, whether in any project it can speak for all its members without coercive influence or downright untruth. To the extent that this local view of the Church is held, resolutions and proceedings of any group cannot profess to be an action of all its members, whether the action be by the parish, or by some national assembly

41

representing the denomination or communion as a whole.

In the following discussion on the work of the Church, the meaning intended is that Christian bodies, however they define the Church, should give serious attention to certain specific matters. Those bodies, such as the Episcopalians and Presbyterians, which hold that a great group of parishes are truly a Church, and those which hold only a local parish is a Church, have their own appropriate methods of bringing their actions and votes and emphases before the rank and file of their members. There is a sense in which any majority vote even in a local parish does represent the will of that group, although it cannot purport to speak for every member.

What are the tasks that lie before the Church?

A. To Preach the Gospel

What is Gospel? What was the message of the Apostles? This is of fundamental importance. In the New Testament there is a clear distinction between preaching and teaching. Teaching involved ethical instruction, the defense of Christianity to the outsider, and the explanation of theological concepts. The Apostolic preaching, on the other hand, was a forthright proclamation to the world. It was based upon accomplished *Christian facts*. Most modern preaching would be teaching in the New Testament sense. In the early Church the Gospel was the announcement of good news, and teaching was in the nature of moral exhortation and explanation. The Church made its converts by the preaching of the Gospel, not by interpretation of it.

The basis of the Gospel is Jesus Christ. Saint Paul in
the classical passage tells us his message to the Corinthians, which was essentially the message of the early
Church.[1] In its leanest form he proclaimed to the Church
at Corinth that Christ died for our sins according to the
Scriptures, that he was buried, that he rose again on the
third day according to the Scriptures, that he was seen by
Cephas. "It was thus that we preached and thus that you
believed." Paul then proceeds to explain some consequences of the acceptance of the message of "Christ and
him crucified." To the Galatians he speaks of Christ
"openly set forth before their eyes as crucified."[2] "He
gave himself for us, to rescue us from the present evil
age."[3] He wrote to the Romans that the word of faith
which he preached was "that Jesus is Lord and that God
raised him from the dead."[4] Paul insisted that the gain-
ing of universal Lordship was the reason for Jesus' death
and resurrection. He added a reference to a Judgment
to come. "We shall all stand before the tribunal of
God."[5] Thus, for Paul, the Gospel based on Christ embraced his resurrection, his lordship, and a Judgment. In
summing up the preaching of Paul, it may be said that
the proclamation was: that prophecy has been fulfilled, a
new age has been started by the advent of Jesus Christ,
that he was born of the seed of David, that he died according to the Scriptures to deliver us from the present evil
age, that he was buried, that he rose on the third day
according to the Scriptures, that he is exalted at the right

---

[1] 1 Cor. 15: 1.
[2] Gal. 3: 1.
[3] Gal. 1: 4.
[4] Rom. 10: 8-9.
[5] Rom. 14: 10.

hand of God, as Son of God and Lord of the quick and the dead, that he will come again as Judge and Savior of mankind. The primitive Gospel as set forth in the Book of the Acts of the Apostles and in the Four Gospels, in spite of numerous small differences, are one in announcing the same Gospel with varied emphases.

Is this what we mean when we say the Church's first duty is to preach the Gospel? Yes, but we mean more. We mean the announcement that God, through Christ, has visited to redeem his people. This involves the facts of Jesus' life, death, and resurrection, his Lordship, and the judgment he brings to men and events. But we also include that which in strict New Testament language is designated "teaching"—ethical instruction, the advocacy of Christianity to the outsider, the explanation of theological concepts, the implication for men and society in an age of immense complexity.

In addition to stating the accomplished facts about Christ, the Church must make clear what he added to the body of spiritual teaching that he received from his forebears. It is entirely compatible with Jesus' spiritual originality that he received much from the prophetic tradition of his people, including insights from Indian, Persian, and Egyptian sources.

Jesus and the early Church were the direct spiritual heirs of the Hebrew prophets. This heritage embraced the ethical standards of Moses (which were not set aside), the idea of a loving God announced by Hosea, the insistent note of social righteousness, the moral heroism of Israel's great leaders, the rich devotional elements of the Psalms, and the accumulated store of religious earnest-

ness built up by the Hebrew people. Jesus was indebted
for his teaching to two sources: the Old Testament; and
to later reflections of Jewish seers contained in such books
as *Ecclesiasticus* and *The Testaments of The Twelve
Patriarchs*. Most of the Gospel utterances may be found
in counterpart in these and other writings by learned
Jewish scholars and teachers. There is no warrant to
believe that Jesus intended to found an ethic entirely
new. He used the best he knew of spiritual life, its obligations and its sanctions.

This is taught by the Church, not as a means of keep-
ing out the unbeliever or the inquirer, but in order to
allow many types to enter. There are teachings that may
not appeal to you or to me. They may not help us to
the main task in life—to know God; but no minister has
an ethical justification for restricting teaching to those
ideas that are most congenial either to him or to his
parishioners. There are other teachings, other doctrines,
that may appeal strongly to others. The custodians of
the Church's life who are enjoined to feed the sheep
must remember there are many varieties within the membership of any parish. Enthusiasm for one aspect of
faith should lead to no neglect of what may be unpalat-
able aspects or areas but slightly explored. God's Spirit
was promised to lead the Church into all the truth.
Patience, a learning and a hospitable mind, and real
Catholicity will help here. The Church has the double
task of making the primitive Gospel of the facts of Jesus
known to the world, and of discovering for itself in days
to come further meanings of that Gospel for men and
society.

Activities that can easily become merely secular and
that are carried on by men of good will may easily lead
the Church to forget its central purpose. The early
Church and all the great periods of its history have been
marked by the sincere proclamation of the Gospel. This
purpose and power is the singular possession of the
Church when it makes plain the fact of Christ, when it
makes clear his teaching, when it invites men to accept
his will as the final arbiter in all their perplexities.

Whenever in a remote mission station, in a backwoods
chapel, or in a great metropolitan center, this witness to
the truth and love of God as it is in Jesus is made plain
and persuasive, there is evidence of spiritual power.
Jesus took the best he found from the past, to which he
added fresh insight. Nevertheless, he taught neither a
revised Jewish morality, nor was he merely preaching a
renewal of the prophetic message—what he took from the
past he made entirely his own and presented it in a
fresh way.

But what is in the truest sense original in Jesus' teaching? There are seven major lines of new teaching. *First,*
Jesus brought a unity to the moral law hitherto unknown.
The Jewish Law and Greek teaching had many precepts
often in conflict with one another; but there is an organic
coherence about Jesus' teaching, consistent throughout.
This organic unity is so marked that anyone acquainted
with Jesus' teaching can recognize whether a given statement is true to his teaching or not. *Second,* morality
in Jesus' mind is derived from a new filial relationship to
God. Man's part is to respond with obedience as a son of
God. Morals and religion are brought together in the

conception that God is made the source of goodness and justice. *Third,* Jesus brought an entirely new emphasis upon the value and dignity of the individual soul. In the Old Testament the nation itself is God's concern and the recipient of God's favor. Although Ezekiel and other later prophets gave larger place to the individual, Jesus was the first to give that attention to man's personality that had formerly been given to the group. *Fourth,* intent is made the determining factor regarding the moral quality of a deed. Jesus deals with the inward life rather than external pretense. *Fifth,* Jesus' ethics are positive in their demands. Negation and restraint are subordinated to the direct command to do. (The accent is on the verb rather than the adjective.) *Sixth,* true morality is separated from external and accidental factors. Jesus disentangled morality from a mass of ceremonial that was smothering it. *Seventh,* in a unique way Jesus, by life and example, gave concrete substance to the moral law. In a true sense he was what he taught.[6]

In its proclamation of the Gospel, the Church must never forget to teach all the lessons and insight the Church has learned. In other words, it must transmit an entire

[6] See Scott, Ernest F., *The Ethical Teachings of Jesus,* Macmillan, New York, 1925, pp. 12-21 ($1.00). Those interested in going more deeply into the subject of the beginnings and work of the early Church can do well to read Bevan, Edwyn, *Christianity,* Holt, New York, 1932 ($1.25), a volume of great clarity and value; Bacon, B. W., *The Founding of the Church,* New York, 1909; Scott, E. F., *The Kingdom of God in the New Testament,* Macmillan, New York, 1931 ($1.75), especially the chapter on "The Church"; Streeter, B. H., *The Primitive Church,* Macmillan, New York, 1929 ($2.50); Lietzmann, Hans, *The Beginnings of the Christian Church,* Scribner, New York, 1937 ($4.00); Dodd, C. H., *The Apostolic Preaching and Its Developments,* London, 1936; Latourette, Kenneth Scott, *The First Five Centuries,* Harper, New York, 1937 ($3.50). See also Lyman, Mary Ely, *Jesus,* in this series.

spiritual culture. This would include what Apostles who were eye witnesses learned from Jesus, as well as what early Church Fathers wrote as their conclusions from life. It would also include statements of subsequent thinkers regarding Jesus and his teaching. To teach a static body of Christian truth is in reality a denial of the continuous revelation God makes of his life through the prophets, through Jesus, and also through Nature, ethics, beauty, the intellect, prayer, conscience, and history in every age. No one of these sources of revelation is to be neglected.

Whenever individuals by a conscious, deliberate choice decide to follow Jesus and to live by his teaching, they enter into a creative fellowship of those who are together seeking that way for themselves and for society. This fellowship in the modern world more nearly approximates the ideal in remote mission stations where medical help, bank credit, seed, and mutual assistance in harvest all center around the Church, as well as worship. In Western civilization the fellowship is often narrowed down to a fellowship of worship only. This fellowship throughout the earth must be enlarged before the Christian faith or Church can effectively spiritualize the world's commerce, politics, and culture.

In preaching the Gospel, the Church must make the Bible understood. With all of its various levels of spiritual value, its stories of crime, its folk lore, Oriental poetry, and tedious and sometimes contradictory chronicles, the Bible is the book of prime importance to the Church, for there we have not only the recital of men's deepest insight, but the story of the life of Jesus Christ.

The Church believes in the Bible not as a magic book but because it contains the record of the dealings of God with men and of man's search for God. It is not the only book that does so, but it is the supreme book of the Christian faith. If men crave a rule, the Ten Commandments are still valid, reinforced by nature and social experience; a code, the Sermon on the Mount, is intact; a way of life, the Golden Rule, is still a way that demands heroism. But they must be applied to life—all of life—to have any significant effect.

B. To Provide a Group Consciousness

An essential task of the Church is to offer friendship within a group that is seeking to follow the teaching and example of Jesus. The more mature the individual, the more he comprehends that this fellowship extends not only to the limits of his local parish but also embraces all believers of every branch of Christendom. No serious person can be self-righteous enough, no person's hands are clean enough, to demand that members of the Church be all spotless and all pure. They are ordinary children of earth, but they are more than a collection of people: they are an organic whole, a household of faith. The arms of the Church should be as wide as the invitation of its Master. It invites those who are seeking to receive and to share spiritual values to throw in their lot with others. There are hypocrites and moth-eaten saints in that membership; there are also broad-minded, clear-headed, and gallant souls. The Church should offer that for which all constructive social forces work—namely, fellowship, a harmonious union of free spirits working together in liberty and order.

Many a man will say, "But what does the Lord or society require of me 'but to do justly, and to love mercy, and to walk humbly with Thy God'?"[7] That is true, but it is not the whole truth. That sentence was written before Jesus Christ was born. It was hard to keep the faith alone, then, and now. No man by himself, no matter how spiritual or how erudite, can know all it means to do justly, to love mercy, and to walk humbly.

No man by himself can know all Christ's meaning for life and society; no man can have insight enough to comprehend all the qualities of Christ. The Spirit of Christ in all its variety of approaches is given to all the members of the Church, not to any one member alone. In any other phase of life—education, politics, economics—men gladly admit the fragmentary nature of their knowledge as individuals. The same principle applies to the profound nature of that spiritual outlook upon life we call religion. Is it not sensible to presume that the whole community of faith may have rich possessions unglimpsed by the individual in his narrow orbit? There is a deep personal meaning in the Gospel, but one cannot know even that personal meaning fully without participating in the whole experience of the whole group.

To preserve and realize fully its own meaning the Church must also develop a historic sense of unity. Just as the insight and experience of the lone individual is too

---

[7]Micah 6: 8.

slender a reed upon which to lean, so the religious consciousness and discoveries of any one generation, sect, or type fail to lead us into all the resources of faith. We enrich the present by laying hold of the past. Ancient Catholic hymns are sung in sectarian congregations, Quaker and Unitarian hymns are used in inclusive "Catholic" bodies such as the Anglican. It is impossible to form a good hymnal without them. Old prayers, hallowed by usage, styles of architecture rich with associations, all the imagery, decoration, and symbolism that have found their way to us by manuscript, textiles, mosaics, wood, stone, glass, enamels, and printing speak of the light that came to other men. Sometimes this is different and other than the illumination which we ourselves have had, and is all the more valuable for that reason. A Church becomes thin and meager unaided by the immense inheritance of other days and other modes. One need not lose oneself in musty medievalism to see the powerful teaching value, the sacramental function of the ideas, the creations, the discoveries of other men of far different racial and cultural background.

A modern man, aware of the solidarity of the peoples of earth, knowing the impossibility of isolating disease, trade depressions, armament races, ideas, or wars, will see that the Church can never fulfill completely, without reunion, its great work of bringing man into personal contact with God. They will not lose themselves in cynicism because Orthodox and Roman Catholic and Anglican and Baptist do not overnight form an organic union, but will with patience take practical steps toward that end. They will see in the Faith and Order Movement, which held its conference at Edinburgh, and in the Life and Work Movement, which met at Oxford in 1937, hopeful signs of an increasing consciousness of the need of unity.

The Protestant Church is always taunted with its divisions, and it is a scandal that they have existed to this date. Not in excuse, but in explanation, one can say we are entering a second historical phase in American Protestantism. Because of the mode of settlement, Dutch, Irish, Scandinavian, Scotch, English, Welsh, German, French, and others brought their national or linguistic churches with them to America. Each year now sees a new phase in the union of various denominations. Significant unions are occurring along the major lines of temperament, taste, and spiritual experience. No good cause could be advanced by offering to men only liturgical or only free churches. There should be appropriate churches for each of the major types.

The cleavages between Low Church and High Church, liberal and fundamental, await the growing tolerance that acknowledges varieties of religious experience—a tolerance already achieved in many large denominations and now dawning in others.

The Church is many, yet one, in its central loyalty, and in its history. The Holy Catholic Church, acknowledged not only by those of the Roman persuasion but by Methodist, Presbyterian, Lutheran, and Quaker alike, is that spiritual unity which is the Church universal, a unity of diversities. Although the names and practice of communions may vary because of historic disagreement and

from variety of practice, nevertheless, there emerges more
to unify than to divide.[8]

The Church derives its life from Jesus Christ and
thereby its essential unity. Although we have the early
churches of the East, such as the Armenians, Nestorians,
and Assyrians, the many national branches of the Orthodox church, the Roman church, and the denominations
of the Protestant world, the Church is still one in the
deepest spiritual sense in that all parts of it acknowledge
Jesus as Lord. Christ is the Head of all of them. However we may divide ourselves, however much we may fall
short of the intelligence, goodness, and spiritual grandeur
of Christ, he makes our unity, he is our one justification
for existence as a corporate fellowship. From Christ
comes everything that is abiding in the Church. He is
the true life of the tiniest parish in the Lebanon Moun-
tains, Yokohama, Melbourne, Paris, or Tanganyika.
White, brown, yellow, black, and red members of scores
of sects and denominations derive their faith, their spiritual life from him. Our unity in him is so much greater
than our divergences of color, class, culture, or ecclesiastical outlook that closer faith, order, life, and work wait
only for the understanding of this unity and courage to
expression it. Our day, in spite of many discouraging
factors, is seeing notable advances toward mutual under-

---

[8] *The Church, Catholic and Protestant,* by William Adams Brown,
Scribner, New York, 1935 ($2.75), is a sound treatment of this whole
subject. *The Spirit of Catholicism,* by Karl Adam, Macmillan, New
York, 1935 ($1.50), is a work by a Catholic scholar of value to Protestants
for the insight it gives into the Catholic way of life, and to the Catholic
for a clear exposition of what his own church teaches. See also *The
Catholic Faith,* by Paul Elmer More, Princeton University Press, Princeton, 1931 ($4.00).

standing among widely variant types of Christian communions.

The second World Conference on Faith and Order, held in Edinburgh in August, 1937, bringing together four hundred and fourteen delegates from one hundred and twenty-two Christian communions in forty-three different countries, unanimously approved the following statement:

We are one in faith in our Lord Jesus Christ. . . . We are one in acknowledging that this allegiance takes precedence of any other allegiance that may make claims upon us.

This unity does not consist in the agreement of our minds or the consent of our wills. It is founded in Jesus Christ Himself. . . .

Our unity is of heart and spirit. We are divided in the outward forms of our life in Christ, because we understand differently His will for His Church. We believe, however, that a deeper understanding will lead us towards a united apprehension of the truth as it is in Jesus.

We humbly acknowledge that our divisions are contrary to the will of Christ, and we pray God in His mercy to shorten the days of our separation and to guide us by His Spirit into fullness of unity.

One reason for divisions in the Church has been the too easy accommodation segments have made to contemporary culture. The Church, often for insufficient reason, has been divided between North and South, rich and poor, black and white. Divergent emphases upon certain elements of early Christianity, human stubbornness and egotism, matters of taste, and impatience with slow-moving groups have multiplied denominations. Some splits have occurred for good reasons; many because of bad temper. In addressing the problem of reunion, Churchmen must, on the one hand, seriously make amends for unjustified divisions, and, on the other, correct abuses that have brought legitimate protests.[9]

As in any group conscious of its life, its dangers, and in a true sense of its privileges, some discipline is necessary in the Church. Weak, unjust, or tyrannical men handle power badly, and make of discipline a source of suffering. Nevertheless, the necessity for order is obvious. But the rules for order and for the sensible carrying forward of work and life must be based upon justice and voluntary acceptance. Order must be rooted in ethical necessity. There can be no continuous group solidarity without some accepted rules by which the group is governed and no free spiritual movement within the Church upon an arbitrary or compulsory basis.

The purpose of all true discipline is to help the individual believer order his life and to liberate him to creative work and thought, to give him a way of life, with direction and help along the way. The individual must not be dragooned or despised or driven; he must be redeemed to orderly and effective life.

Continuity, authority, common belief, and loyalty are the conditions of the organic life of groups. Evelyn Underhill discerns these factors at work in the life of the Church: *first,* a body of tradition; *second,* an authoritative organization through which teaching can be transmitted, including an order of ministers or its equivalent; *third,* an acknowledged common interest, such as a be-

---

[9] See Niebuhr, H. Richard, *The Social Sources of Denominationalism,* Holt, New York, 1929 ($2.50). Although this volume does not deal exhaustively with some valid causes of division, it is a devastating analysis of the fragile reasons which have too often led groups to form new sects.

lief, an idea, or a creed; and *fourth,* hostile conditions that develop loyalty. "We find ourselves, then, committed to the picture of a Church or spiritual institution that is in essence Liturgic, Ecclesiastical, Dogmatic, and Militant, as best fulfilling the requirements of group psychology. Four decidedly indigestible morsels for the modern mind, yet, group-feeling demands some common expression if it is to be lifted from notion to fact. Discipline requires some authority and some devotion to it. Culture involves a tradition handed on. And there, we said, were the chief gifts the institution had to give to its members."[10] One of the Church's primary tasks is to build up a group consciousness.

C. To Provide Adequate Worship

The Church also has the duty of providing occasions of worship cast in significant and beautiful forms in both liturgical and non-liturgical services. The non-liturgical as well as the more formal communions have done much in making more adequate the celebration of the goodness and the love of God which is the essential act of worship. Within the formal and the informal modes of worship, and within combinations and variations of the two, there is opportunity for differing taste and religious experience to find expression and sustenance for spiritual life. There in a social factor in worship with a group that is not attained alone, as desirable as are private devotions. The presence of others at a service is a reinforcement that everyone sorely needs.

---

[10] Underhill, Evelyn, *The Life of the Spirit and the Life of Today,* Dutton, New York, 1922, p. 164   ($2.50).

Whether a Church be Catholic-minded and liturgical, or separatist and free in its worship, its main task is always to mediate the life of God to men. Those who incline to placing the major emphasis upon worship and the Sacraments, rather than upon preaching, feel that special rites, special times, special seasons, help focus attention, and make all food and drink, all work, and all reasons more significant. Quakers and Salvationists may disregard the Sacraments; but, in fact, they have chosen other Sacraments—silence and a close, deeply moving fellowship of a dedicated group.

The Church's plain duty is to employ every appropriate method to make the administration of the Sacraments available, beautiful, and significant. Churches that administer the Lord's Supper too infrequently engender a coldness toward it. Churches that have Holy Communion each Sunday run the danger of falling into a purely formal habit. Only great care and religious feeling can preserve every value and prevent the Sacraments from becoming commonplace. Liturgical Churches here have a great advantage over free Churches—a situation that can only be remedied by an even greater insight and care by the latter. Men have a perennial need of renewal. The Sacraments to large areas of men bring that fresh increment of cleansing strength which they need. A Communion service is not an ordered argument such as the sermon in a sense must be. It is an individual as well as a corporate act of worship. He receives most who brings himself as an offering. Our task at such a service is primarily, to come, to partake, to remember.

As the Church contemplates its duty, it must never forget that one of its main endeavors of providing adequate worship must be to aid man in achieving his supreme duty—union with God; we are aware of God as personal, making his absolute ethical demands and offering his help.

This is done through a cultus that may be very simple, as with the Quakers, or elaborate, as with the Roman church. By Sacraments, by corporate suggestion, by its discipline, its symbols, its songs, its Scripture, its acts of worship all directed to celebrate God in his fulness, this secret is imparted. By giving oneself to these factors and practices we are powerfully addressed by the grace of God. Our task is to come, to give attention, to offer ourselves, to be sympathetic; otherwise, like an inflexible person before art or music, we are *profane* in the old Latin sense—that is, outside the temple. Services of worship, liturgy, song, the motions of the body in kneeling, bowing the head, or approaching the Communion rail are powerful helps to put the mind in that state of receptivity wherein the deeper aspects of prayer and devotion are possible. Through developing an artistic expression, the Church rightly utilizes suggestion to present our resources and our obligations, while at the same moment it reinforces our memory with images of what we are dedicating ourselves to accomplish.

Fundamentally, the process of achieving union with God lies in imitating Jesus Christ. This is the primary function not only of sincere members but of the Christian Church in its corporate capacity. If the Church is realistically to live up to its spiritual title as the Body of Christ it must do what Jesus did, be what he was. It must go out as a teacher, a healer, a fisherman, a shepherd, even as he. It must have love, honor, grace, truth, compassion, deep in its bones, expressed in its speech, active in all works that increase faith and heal men and society.

D. TO HELP MEN REALIZE THEIR FULLEST SPIRITUAL STATURE

1. *In Relation to Their Own Nature*

The Church must always be interested in the care and cure of souls, in helping men to realize their fullest life on every personal and social plane. Before any adequate social order can be made, sound men must be created. Over and beyond our national and community and family needs (but not blinding us to them) there stands the solitary man, one of the great facts of the universe. In his terrible isolation, even when crowded by associates, he needs help—for body, mind, and spirit. He needs refreshment for his emotions, reinforcement for his will, added truth to stabilize and enrich his intelligence.

Four definite tasks lie before the Church in building up the inner life of men. *First,* to enable men to achieve full intellectual and emotional adulthood. Modern education and psychology have given immense new resources, which the Church must employ in helping men, women, and children rid themselves of adult infantalism in the achievement of maturity. *Second,* to bring spiritual influence to bear upon home, school, and industry to enable men to achieve self-support. *Third,* through conference, literature, and personal counseling, to assist the young to grow naturally, normally, and effectively in a world of men and women. A sane idea of the relationships between boys and girls and men and women, the teaching of sound ideals of courtship and marriage and the birth and rearing of children, are vital needs of our civilization. We have today as we have never had before a body of information and literature, as well as specialists in the field, which is available to any parish. *Fourth,* to help all its members to develop a philosophy of life that sees realistically all the compromised relationships with which any life is surrounded and yet to achieve a way of life, wherein they may approximate as much as possible to the standards of Jesus.

If men are to realize their fullest life, care must be exercised to encourage prophetic and reforming spirits. Whenever men and women labor for the aims of Jesus, whether they be in the Church or not, whether their means of expression are those customarily employed by the Church, and even when they are violently hostile to the Church, the truth within their speech and programs must be accounted as in line with the will of God. This requires no little Christian grace, for often men intolerant of religious institutions carry forward projects that the Church has lacked vision or courage to set in motion. Many deeply spiritual men feel that the secular religions, such as communism, are playing the same rôle on the stage of history that nations of the East played in the life of Israel. They are being used to flail a Church that has lost its idea of the dignity and value of man, its awareness of human need, and its faith in divine resources, into fresh eagerness to do its task. Artists, novelists, play-

wrights, manufacturers, politicians can often do a work
impossible for clergymen.

2. *In Their Relation to the Home*

No collective to which the individual belongs has
greater importance than the family. Here is the psychical
matrix in which the intellectual and emotional patterns
of men receive their early and, in most cases, permanent
conditioning. One need not be a fatalist to recognize
the powerful pressures that mold life for good or ill
within the home.

The home cannot be protected by a merely negative
ethic, by prohibitions, or by inhibitive ideals. No sound
morality issues from either coercion or fear. The room
that is swept and garnished is soon inhabited by seven
other spirits or habits worse than the ones that have been
driven out. The new freedom of modern times has
brought evil with it necessarily, but it has brought a
knowledge of the inner life, which, reinforced by
Christian regard for personality, can make modern homes
different and better than we have ever known. Commercialized amusement, automobiles, the freer talk
about sex, the widespread knowledge of birth control,
must be faced realistically. That portion or that use of
modern institutions and practices which are un-Christian
can better be met by substitution of worthy uses and
ideas than by any amount of condemnation.

3. *In Their Relation to the Community*

We find ourselves inevitably immersed in various collectives or human groupings that partake of the nature of

both good and evil. We cannot follow the Stoic's doctrine, "If the house smokes, leave it." The whole meaning of Christ coming to earth to live as a normal man amid sinful and compromised groups is that God means us to redeem men and society by opposing love, honor, and sacrifice to hatred, dishonesty, and self-seeking. One of the collectives in which we are entangled is the community.

Particularly, the Church by its very nature as a divine institution is charged with the guarding of men from claims of infallibility or ultimate supremacy by the community. Again, the Church accepts racial groups as one means God employs to enrich the life of humanity by diverse insights, experiences, and talents. The Christian ethic is unalterably against all racial pride or persecution, and recognizes the responsibility to achieve racial equality first in its own membership.

There are many factors in community life that demand for their solution the highest intelligence and willingness to sacrifice on the part of Christian people. Every parish has a problem to realize in its own self a true unity transcending all class, race, and financial barriers. Every parish also has a problem in achieving active collaboration with all other parishes in its district. The underprivileged, the outcast, the depressed still knock at the door of every church. But charity must never be allowed to substitute for active efforts to change existing conditions, such as the tension between the youth and age, between men and women, disease, bad housing, unemployment, unjust economic conditions, such as wages un-

bearably low, unworthy recreation, and the critical problem of enabling youth to find a true vocation. No better
laboratory can be offered than the parish for undertak-
ing new social experiments. No device is better able to
lift the conscience of the people. The Church has an
immense service to render as a reconciler in the strife
between members of families, the eternal struggle between the citizen and his government. No better
auspices can be found for careful study of the vexed problems of our generation. Members of churches should be
actively encouraged to take responsibility in local and
national government, and to put Christian principles into
the texture of our economic and political life. The
Church has still the hard problem of inducing men,
women, and children voluntarily to discipline themselves
in taste, in manners, and in all forms of self-indulgence.
No parish can achieve its fullest life until it raises the life
of the community to the level of the Christian ethic. As
a segment of the universal fabric of Christendom, it must
recognize itself as a part of the world-wide Church and
lend aid to make the world community truly Christian.[11]

4. *In Their Relation to the State*

Another collective in which we find our lives enmeshed
is the state in its governmental aspect. Here too we find
an institution which, in the New Testament sense, is
ordained of God. Here too we find the good and the bad
mixed together. Here too we may be grateful for the

---

[11] See *The Message and Decisions of Oxford on Church, Community
and State*, New York, 1937, pp. 12-13 ($.25).

immense benefits the state has brought us. Society would be hopeless anarchy unless the state carried forward orderly administration. To say that the state deserves criticism and should be opposed for any injustice to personality is far different from the attitude of some Christians who would hold that the state is a sinful institution and therefore should be no concern of the Church. That way lies anarchy. The state is secular, its ultimate sanction is force, but it is necessary as one of the fundamental orders of life. The Church must recognize the state in its own area as the highest authority. Every theocracy where the Church has taken over the functions of the civil state has ended in disaster through immersing the Church in a maze of secular administration, diverting its talent, and swamping its leadership in inevitable compromise. The Church does its best work within states, by exercising a critique of the state's ways and by constantly pointing to better modes of government. The Church must always insist that, even as itself, the state is accountable to God.

Members of the Church are related to their states through the people for whom the state is the political organ. Thus, the duties of the Church to the state are in some measure determined by all the aspects of the social, economic, and cultural life of man. The state, because of its monopoly of the means of coercion, can easily become an instrument of evil. For the Church, God is the source of justice, whereas the state is the guarantor of the liberties of men. "It is not the Lord, but the servant of justice." The state therefore has a twofold relationship to the Church: first, as an order within which Christians have to live; and, second, as an institution which may either promote or retard the work of the Church.[12]

The Church and Christian people generally owe certain duties to the state. The Church should not only pray for the right administration of government but also use its influence to aid all ethical measures intiated by the state for the common good. It should give obedience to the state except where laws or policies are contrary to Christian teaching. Then it must disobey. It has a positive duty to offer criticism whenever the state departs from the Christian ethic. It should always keep before legislators and administrators those principles that make for the realization of the whole nature and dignity of man. It should permeate public life with the spirit of Christ and train citizens who as Christians can aid in making the whole social fabric more Christian.[13] The Church should denounce the use of coercive power by the state in regard to religion. Membership in a minority Church should never be a reason for denying full civil and political equality.

Certain liberties are essential to the Church before it can fulfill the duties which are laid upon it by God and man. There must be liberty to determine faith and creed, public and private worship, liberty of preaching and of teaching. It is the plain duty of the Christian to oppose the state whenever it seeks to prescribe religious ceremonies or forms of worship. Liberty to make its own government and to lay down qualifications for its clergy and its membership must be inviolable, as well as free-

[12] *Ibid.,* pp. 25-26.
[13] *Ibid.,* p. 28.

dom of the individual to join the Church of his choice. The Church cannot fulfill its primary functions unless it be free to educate its ministers and its young, to carry on missionary activity at home and abroad, to co-operate with other Churches within the nation and throughout the world to own property and to collect funds.

In many lands these conditions are violated in whole or in part. The Christian Church that is dedicated to build up man to his true stature, which is perfectly exemplified in Christ, must use its strength, even if at great sacrifice, to protect men from the actions of over-zealous states.

5. *In Their Relation to the Economic Order*

In days gone by the Church has often had blood upon her hands. She has ostracized many who have struggled against social injustice. This has been a tragic blunder. The Church must provide hospitality for many restless, enthusiastic, and often inconvenient souls, realizing that the tendency of any institution is to become conservative and even reactionary. The energies of many outside the Church who see the world's pain must be led into channels of spiritual usefulness or they will run amuck in unreasoned iconoclasm. The Church in its relationship to labor has too often estranged or condemned suppressed classes because they have presented their need in uncouth ways. Turning a deaf ear to legitimate hope breeds violence. Neither communism nor fascism can grow without a seedbed of unrest and resentment to feed upon.

Overconcentration of wealth, greed, slums, war, disease, poverty, the abuses of liquor and drugs, the traffic in women, and tyranny in various forms beset every nation. In most cases these social diseases have an economic basis. Christian people can never cease to lay the injustice and needs on the conscience of mankind, at the same time furnishing an adequate means by which the public conscience may express itself. The normal needs of men for love, home, food, shelter, and work must be satisfied. The Church must not only do its part but stimulate the state and the community to do their part. Mark Twain said, "Principles have no real force except when one is well fed." The Church's task here is twofold: *first,* to create a desire for just changes in the life of man and society; and, *second,* to provide a technique that will be the instrument of that will. We know enough now to make society immensely better, but secular leadership and the Church alike are still seeking an adequate technique of social change.

The Church insists that all the institutions that affect life should increasingly be brought under the Spirit of Christ. Anything that fails to respect man as the child of God, made in his image, comes under its judgment. Love and Christian charity must never substitute for hard, honest effort on the part of the Church to make the whole framework of commerce Christian.

The Church, on the one hand, must avoid the error of indiscriminate condemnation of business men, practices, and institutions; and, on the other, it cannot identify or equate any social system with the Kingdom of God. Paradoxically, the Kingdom of God both has come and is coming. It came in Jesus Christ as an accomplished historical fact. It has yet to come in society. To deny any good in the efforts of honest business men and honest labor leaders to improve commerce is to deny the reality of the Kingdom in history. To identify any social system with the Kingdom is to equate the Kingdom with what necessarily is a long, painful, historical process.

Every economic order today challenges the Church's deepest life by acquisitiveness, by widespread inequalities that in themselves deny a fair chance to millions, by concentration of economic power in a few hands, all of which so conditions life that it is impossible for most men to achieve a sense of Christian vocation. Primary needs of food, clothing, and shelter force many into work that may either be socially useless or into such forms of effort as "pressure selling," which may have serious consequences, economic and moral, for both seller and buyer.

There are certain factors in our economic life that lie within the area of the Church's work. Because the Church should deal with ends or goals, it is often accused of losing its true force in generalities. But it deals with large areas of men in various situations. It must lay down principles by which concrete situations are to be tested.

There are five standards that apply to any economic situation. *First,* any economic system that frustrates the life of individuals or divides men into classes based upon wealth or position, or that breeds a sense of injustice among the less privileged, is un-Christian and should be changed. *Second,* every child must have training for the development of his capacities and must be given as far as possible that measure of health, wholesome environment, and family life that will aid him in his preparation for life work. *Third,* those disabled should receive just and merciful care. *Fourth*, labor should never be considered as a commodity. Men should be free and able to recognize and fulfill a Christian vocation. A living wage, a wholesome environment, and a voice in the decisions that affect his life should be achieved and safeguarded for the worker. *Fifth,* there must be a recognition of man's trusteeship before God, for all the fruit of the earth demands radical curbing or waste on farms, in factories, and in our mineral resources.

These five standards imply definite modifications of our economic life that the Church and society must recognize. It must be acknowledged that property rights are relative. God is the giver of all wealth; He is the creator of man's abilities to develop the fruitage of the earth. This Christian conviction must express itself in the idea of trusteeship. The Christian must examine his property in the light of its social consequences.

The Church must first turn its scrutiny upon itself to reshape its own institutional life along truly Christian lines. It has done much and can do more to develop technique and machinery for research and action. Most difficult of all, it must achieve an effective unity between work and worship, between Sunday and the six days of labor. In this task the widest possible liberty should be given for individuals, for groups in local parishes, for denominational commissions and Church federations, locally, nationally, and internationally, to experiment with courage.

6. *In Their Relation to Education*

The Church is essentially a fellowship of free persons

seeking to bring all men under the transforming influence of Christ. It recognizes no divisions of nation, race, or class. It is also an eternal fellowship viewing men not only as citizens in relation to contemporary communities and states, but also as citizens of an ongoing spiritual order, and therefore it necessarily demands more in the way of education than is demanded by any state to fit its citizens for their purely secular duties.

The state is primarily concerned with the general intelligence of its citizens, upon which rests the business and administrative fabric of its life. Its object is to produce a loyal and efficient people. National solidarity is especially desired in a day of social disintegration. In states with large liberties, the right of other agencies to participate in education is recognized. The community through its institutions, enthusiasms, ideals, and prejudices is a potent educational factor, far stronger than the use of any formal methods. Tendencies within community or state to dehumanize man must be resisted.

What is the task and purpose of the Church in education? It is twofold. *First,* it must do all in its power to secure for every citizen the widest opportunity for the development and use of his talents. *Second,* it has a special responsibility in education dealing with man's responsibility to God. It must always uphold its right to educate its own children, admitting the state right to set standards of general education for citizenship. In education the Church faces one of its sharpest conflicts with totalitarian governments.

Various factors in the contemporary scene complicate

the relations between community, Church, and state. The secularization of life, an overconfident belief in man's ability to direct his own destiny, social decay, the loosening of home loyalties, the attempt to mold the minds of pupils to some preconceived pattern in the interest of a party, a government or an ideology, the influence of the radio and moving pictures, and the increasing intervention of states has set up inevitable tensions between the state and all other agencies working in the educational field.

Certain crucial issues are before the Church and Christians generally in regard to education. Freedom is by no means assured in any land, and in many it has been taken away. Without true liberty no worthy system of education is possible. Men's minds are either warped or denied the growth that is their birthright. The Church is necessarily hostile to the zealous and often violent integrating processes by which modern states seek to unify their disintegrating peoples. The Church with its fellowship that recognizes no division of nations, class, or color finds itself the center of attack in such situations. The control of youth movements in the interest of secular partisan ideals is directly contrary to the Church's conviction about the education of the young and the inviolability of personality. A one-sided education directed toward employment alone, which excludes the possibility of training the whole man, is a matter of grave concern. The Church will do well not only to welcome the immense enlargement of life that has come through modern knowledge, method, and technique, but also to keep its own educational services equal in every way to the best theory and practice in the field of education.

Certain tasks of immediate and pressing importance rest upon the Church. A body of philosophical and theological thought adequate not only to combat modern error but to capture the best intellect for the cause of Christ must be developed and made easily accessible. A philosophy and a psychology of distinctively Christian education must be formulated. It is also imperative that the Church perform more effectively her own educational function among children, young people, and adults as well as aid government agencies in all means within her power.

The Church has *one unique contribution* to make to the education of the race—the Gospel. As never before men need an interpretation of their own nature, of God, of the person and work of Jesus Christ, of the meaning of life itself. Unless they are to flounder in endless wars and misery men must achieve a world view, give a meaning to men's lives, a sense of destiny and an experience of divine resources, which alone can save us from the sub-human and demonic influences that seem always waiting to engulf the best as well as the worst civilizations.

7. *In Their Relation to the World of Nations*

The Church finds her life amid a family of nations. She neither can nor should desire escape from such an existence. She recognizes proper areas for the operation of governments other than those of her own nation, even as she recognizes an area in which the state is the supreme authority. Although she does not equate the Kingdom of

God with any present or conceivable international order, she does insist that men make choices within the present order that make for peace and human betterment. The state, whether it recognizes the fact or not, is not autonomous but is under the ultimate rule of God. There is an important distinction between the responsibility of states and that of the individual. The individual is more free to sacrifice his life than the state is to spill the blood of her citizens. The state is a trustee of the life and well-being of all its subjects. Thus, the individual is freer to choose his path than is the state.

Whereas a state represents a union between law and force, in international relations law and force have never been made effective. The various sister states stand side by side without any organic union and without any adequate international law. The claim of each state to unrestricted sovereignty, to be judge of its own cause, is the most effective stumbling block to an ethical international order. The power-relationship undisciplined by effective international law is in itself un-Christian.

The Church has a positive duty to aid all attempts toward peace without identifying any one method or means as the sole or only hope of an ethical international order. Lovers of peace could do well to scrutinize the strength and the weakness of the League of Nations, and give thought toward strengthening its structure. They must give support to the Permanent Court of International Jutice, to just treaties, and to efforts by the various branches of the Church to bring about a just division of the earth's resources to the end that the "haves" shall not exploit the "have nots."

The most pressing aspect of international life and the outstanding social sin of our generation is war. Upon no subject have Christian men given more thought—and as yet they have achieved no unanimity of opinion. Certain attitudes are sincerely held by different members in nearly every parish. *First,* a large number of both clergy and laymen take the attitude that modern war is such that no Christian should have any part in it. This is the full pacifist position. It should be respected wherever sincerely held by both Church and government. *Second,* many sincere Christians assert that there are "just wars." Two points of view emerge here, depending upon the definition of what constitutes a "just war": (a) To vindicate international law by force, in the same manner that the police within a state would vindicate local civil and criminal law. Most of those holding this point of view would say that no war would be just if the state concerned fails to submit the dispute to arbitration. (b) To defend the victims of aggression or to secure liberty for those who are being tyrannized. Where all other devices fail, it is then thought proper to resort to war. Those holding this point of view assert that the individual Christian who may be willing to sacrifice himself cannot ethically expose others by declining to fight for them.[14] No one of these opinions can be held as the only Christian position. The very confusion that exists upon the subject is a tragic revelation of the wholesale social sin in which the Church is enmeshed. Often the choice is by no means a clear one between good and evil, but between two evils.

---

[14] *Ibid.,* pp. 83-84.

Whenever the Church is caught up in a situation involving tension between neighbor states, it can do no less than generate and maintain love, reject hatred, and remove racial barriers in society and in its own life. It must retain at all costs, and aid fellow believers to maintain, freedom of assembly, of worship, and of missionary endeavor. It must promote mutual aid among all branches of Christendom, teach men the universal nature of the Church itself, maintain realistic peace education, and pioneer in discovering ways to achieve an ethical order among the family of nations. It must both inform itself concerning armament and disarmament, and with all other branches of the Christian faith seek to achieve a united voice and action to promote harmony among all men, to the end that man may achieve his true destiny as a human being and as a child of God. Much work of great value is being carried forward in this field by Church Commissions. The Church is uniquely fitted to be a sounding board for a more critical attitude toward war for both pacifist and non-pacifist. This disunity of the Church before the threat of imminent war is nothing short of a spiritual tragedy.

E. To Realize Its Own True Nature as the Body of Christ

At its best the Church knows the necessity of being susceptible to further teaching—that it must follow added light. From the beginning there has been a conflict in the Church between primitivism and growth. The advocate of primitivism conceives Christianity in terms of an essence. Anything lacking this essence is for him not

Christian. This essence is to be found in the New Testament. It is the religion of Jesus defined in the leanest terms. The advocate of growth holds that such an essence cannot be separated from the processes of life. Growth is the law of life, and Christianity is a living thing; therefore, it too must grow. Forcing Christianity back into New Testament molds would stop its development and eventually kill it. The advocate of growth asserts that anything is Christian that bears the name and is in the main current of historic tradition.

The primitivist view would tend to kill the Christian faith by denying growth, whereas the advocate of growth would tend to suffocate it by discouraging reform. Christianity must grow to live. The Church must realize that change and adaptation are inherent in growth. If the adaptation go too far, the original pattern may be forever lost. However, any organism may become diseased and be in need of drastic surgery. Here again the two major conceptions of what the Church is come into play. Those who hold the Church is an inclusive fellowship are willing to accommodate, to borrow, and to adapt. The danger is that the original leaven be lost in the huge lump. The sect type is more concerned to live after the primitive pattern. In doing this it frequently develops a meager life by refusing to partake of the value of an on-going experience.

The Protestant world is now embarked on one of the most significant enterprises it has ever undertaken—that of realizing its own universal nature. The World Conference of Life and Work at Oxford and the World Conference on Faith and Order in Edinburgh in the summer of 1937, issuing in a World Council of Churches, bids fair to achieve a universal voice for Protestantism, a benefit long enjoyed by the Roman communion. When and if a greater union shall be achieved between Protestantism and Catholicism, no man knows. We can only hope that Christians can so live that an atmosphere can be created in which better relations may grow and ripen. We must bear in mind that the nature of Christendom is not international, but ecumenical. The word international accepts the division of mankind into separate nations. The word ecumenical denotes the accomplished fact within history of the unity of the Church in Christ, which knows no frontiers.

Along with greater realization of its own true nature comes the insistent conviction that the Church's major task is the Christianizing first of itself, then of the whole world on every personal and social plane. In obedience to its own deepest loyalty to Christ, the Church has carried on an effort to evangelize the world. Far-flung missionary endeavors embrace preaching, teaching, agriculture, trade schools, translations, literature, medicine, sanitation, public health, and scores of services calculated to benefit the body, mind, and spirit of man. The missionary labors of the last century constitute a spiritual expansion unique in history. Many union projects, joint endeavors through the International Missionary Council, and other union and federated bodies give encouragement to those who wish the Church as a whole to share the best God has given with all who need. These enterprises undertaken as a common task help the Church to realize its own true estate as the Body of Christ.

How is the Church to accomplish the work to which by its very nature it is committed—the Christianizing of the individual, the home, the community, the state, the family of nations?

There is great need to recruit able, courageous, and enlightened men and women for its leadership, train them at the best colleges, universities, and seminaries, and send them forth fearless of the face of man to preach the Gospel and to bury their lives in the life of towns, cities, and rural parishes. These men and women must have brains, physical stamina, imagination, sensitivity, a friendly nature, a philosophical background, and a loyalty to Christ that will enable them to deal effectively with the complicated modern scene. Only the best should be claimed for this service.

Numbers of adequately prepared specialists in psychiatry, religious education, sex instruction, economics, and sociology, are necessary to keep the Church keen to danger and responsibility and at the same time save it from ill-advised or foolish action.

A larger enlistment of laity than has ever before existed is necessary. Modern methods, machines, and corporate management have vastly enlarged the ability of men to extend their influence, and at the same time has given an anonymity that is dangerously removing the personal element in business. Unless the Church is to be a small minority of pietist souls, it must with courage apply the Gospel in the politics and industry and finance of our day. This can be done only by laymen.

More cross-fertilization of ideas from different groups and denominations would do much to enrich Church life.   Surely the Church's faith is strong enough to expose its most cherished tastes, traditions, and policies to the combined scrutiny of the ablest and most sensitive minds of Christendom.   The tedium of Conferences and joint committees may gladly be endured for the sake of mutual enrichment.   Every parish may thereby attain the sense of being an organic part of Christendom.

The realization that the local parish, the family, and the individual are the materials out of which Christendom is built is a pressing need.   In the families and in the year-round work of the congregation, clergy and laity must approximate as far as is humanly possible the Christian ideal, both personally and socially.   Imagination, intelligence, courage, and faith are the watchwords of the Church for the day that is upon us.

CHAPTER V

THE CHURCH IN ACTION—FOUR METAPHORS USED BY JESUS

Jesus employed four metaphors—the figures of the fisherman, the teacher, the healer, and the shepherd—in describing the operation of the grace of God, and gave a sure indication of what their work was to be.

A. THE FIGURE OF THE FISHERMAN

The Church is made up of men and women, of boys and girls. How does it secure these people? Some are born into the Church. They come from Christian families, they are reared in Sunday school, they attend Church services proper and never know themselves to be different. Many have a feeling for worship and maintain an allegiance to the Church in adult years, partly through habit, partly through sincere conviction. But the greater part of society is without the confines of this group; a few are definitely hostile; some join and break away; many pay respect but do not come; the vast majority care little for the Church or its services. They do not hate or love the Church; they are simply not concerned in any vital way.

Individual parishes would tend to die out unless members were constantly recruited. Why make the effort? Let me reply as one who believes in the Church.

We make the effort for several imperative reasons. *First,* we seek to be obedient to the plain teachings of

Jesus Christ. For him the race was a family; it was not composed of mutually antagonistic groups or indiviudals. This view was based upon Jesus' profoundly realistic scrutiny of our entire human situation. He knew that no man could either live or die alone. How true this has been proved by war, depression, and pestilence within ~~the~~ lifetime of ~~those who read this book.~~ *our*

Second, we make the effort in response to a deep impulse within us to share the best we have. Contrary to the idea that the whole fabric of individual and social life is based upon selfishness, either dull or enlightened, men do give ideas, food, medicine, counsel, shelter, clothing to their friends in need. Is it any wonder that they cannot help sharing the love, the intelligence, and the compassion that they found in so extraordinary a person as Jesus?

Third, we make the effort out of sheer loyalty to the idea of sportsmanship. Everything that we have in life which is of value, whether it be of material things, of scientific import, of esthetic appreciation or of spiritual insight, has come to us from dozens and even hundreds of sources. Our fathers' fathers, even as ourselves, are under a debt we can never pay to unknown men whose skills and insights, whose techniques and labors have contributed to our life and well-being.

Fourth, we make the effort in fidelity to the Gospel itself that we believe to be truth (and by truth we mean a direct correspondence to the nature of things as they are). If the Gospel is true, then it is true for all. Medical truth, mathematical truth, historical truth cannot be segregated. It is for all. So is spiritual truth. We shall not enjoy the full fruits of medicine until every land be free from undernourishment, tuberculosis, small-pox, and venereal disease. We shall not know the full fruits of the spiritual truth revealed in Christ and in the lives of the best of his followers until every tongue and tribe know and appropriate and live by that truth.

The critic or the inquirer might ask himself, "But how shall the priest, the minister, or a layman of a local parish do this work of recruiting?" Let me be as simple and concrete as possible. My experience as a minister would not be profoundly different from that of other clergymen or laymen who are sincerely interested in the Church. An usher tells me of some new family that has come to town. I call upon them. If they have children, I tell them about our church school. Some friend says he has a man or a woman working for him. I call upon that person and explain what we are attempting to do at our church; or if such a person belongs to another denomination, I put him or her in touch with the priest or minister of that parish. An emigrant family settles on a neighborhood street. I visit them and acquaint them with books in their language in our local library; I put them in touch with people who know their speech. I meet people upon trains, in buses, in hospital wards and rooms, sometimes through letters, or in short conversations after a service. At weddings and funerals and baptisms, as a servant of the Church, I see a varied company. My task in life is to interest them, not in myself, or in the local parish as an entity in itself, but in Christ and in the work of the Christian Church as the Body of Christ—Christendom. But because we only have denominations through which to work, I seek to interest them either in my parish or in that of a neighboring colleague.

Dozens of us in the clergy make from a thousand to twelve hundred personal and family calls each year. We know we must serve as best we can the families already in our parish, but must always be going out as fishers of men in every decent and appropriate way to interest and persuade and convince men that the Christian Church is the greatest enterprise in the world; that as weak as it may be, as abused as it has been by tawdry or ignorant or tyrannical men, it is one of the chief instruments of God to mediate His grace to men.

"Come ye after me and I will make you fishers of men." This is no idle invitation. It is meant for the clergy, and no less for the sincere layman and lay woman. You will recall that Andrew quickly went to call Simon his brother. In long midnight walks, in conversation with roommates, in consultation in the study, in the deep and intimate converse of friend with friend, the testing point and the crisis of the Christian faith occurs at this critical juncture: when you and I have the courage and the love to invite our comrades not to faith in us but to faith in and devotion to Jesus as Lord, to trust in his mind, and to devotion to his spirit.

B. THE FIGURE OF THE TEACHER

At the very beginning the primitive Christian communities knew our Lord face to face, or were instructed by those who had seen him and heard him speak, but as individuals went out to other groups in Palestine, Egypt, Galatia, Greece, Macedonia, Italy, Spain, and Gaul, and as their children grew up, teaching became a necessary function of the Church. Many of the Church's ablest minds since Apostolic days have given themselves to this work. The Church's teaching function applies to all issues that directly affect the life of men, their wives, and their children.

There are several major lines of teaching vitally needed today when men sincerely want and actually need the light of Christian teaching on problems that are torturing their minds.

One line of teaching has to do with social relationships. Where Christ's spirit prevails in parishes we see free pews and a more friendly spirit take the place of a rather hard exclusiveness. Those who are poor and wear shabby clothes are made to feel that their contribution is as valuable as those who are able to give large amounts. I have had families giving thirty-five cents for important funds, an amount that certainly in God's eyes was as valuable as thousands of dollars that rich men and women have also generously given. The Church needs to make its own social life right, but it dare not stop with itself. Many clergymen and laymen are doing much to create better social conditions. Enlightened churchmen are teaching that labor has a right to discuss wages and hours, to have some reasonable share in the control of conditions of work, some assurance of security in old age, the right to collective bargaining, freedom of speech, the right to strike, and the right to work—and that power of any kind brings with it a corresponding responsibility.

Another line of necessary teaching inherent in the Christian faith involves our attitude toward race prejudice, the demoniacal character of lynchings, the injustice of economic or social discrimination toward men of another color. We are only beginning to see the essentially sub-Christian character of our historic treatment of the American Negro. It is easy to assume a correct attitude in the abstract, but we know that the test of conviction regarding race relations comes with the Negroes and Chinese and Japanese and Jews of the town in which we live.

The status of women and children legally, and in the matter of wages, is still far below a just level. Thousands of able women do as much or more than men in various callings for less than one-half the wage. Child labor is still a blot on the Western World. As a servant of the Church I have exposed five sweat shops employing children below working years for more than sixty hours a week at a wage of less than three dollars. Many of my colleagues have done distinguished service in behalf of women and children.

It might be felt by the layman who is not fully aware of the facts that the Church has been laggard regarding the international relations and contacts. This may be true, but in some respects a great work has nevertheless been done. To name only a few of the actual co-operative works of the Church in these fields may be of interest. The World Christian Student Federation unites Student Christian Movements in fifty nations. It collects information regarding religious conditions among students. Through varied forms of leadership it attempts to persuade students to become sincere followers of Jesus Christ, to develop their spiritual life, and to enlist them in the work of extending the margins of Christendom.

The Church Peace Union carries on work throughout the world in the interest of peace. The World Alliance for International Friendship through the Churches has done much to organize religious forces of the Protestant world in order that their united influence may be brought to bear upon the relations of governments and of peoples in the interest of good will and of peace. The World's Committees of the Young Men's and of the Young Women's Christian Associations have performed a notable labor in the interest of international friendship. The Universal Christian Council for Life and Work and the World Conference on Faith and Order have brought together the leading churchmen of the world to discuss common problems both of a practical and a philosophical nature. During the conferences in Oxford and Edinburgh in 1937 plans were developed for an early organization of a World Council of Churches.

The World's Christian Endeavor Union and the World's Sunday School Association are two practical efforts for training youth and leaders of youth. The International Missionary Council brings together the best minds in many missionary organizations throughout the world to prevent duplication, to discover better methods, and to plan effective occupation of areas as yet untouched by the Christian forces.

The International Congregational Council, the Ecumenical Methodist Conferences, the Lambeth Conference of Bishops, the World Alliance of the Reformed Churches Holding the Presbyterian Systems, and other international denominational bodies bring together several branches of Christendom for mutual support and counsel.

The Federal Council of Churches of Christ in America, through its departments of Evangelism, Church and Social Service, Race Relations, Radio, Research and Education, International Justice and Good Will, Relations with Churches Abroad, and Worship, and its various committees and commissions, has enabled many segments of the divided Protestant forces of America to develop a sense of unity in practical work and service. All of these efforts are part of the teaching function of the Church issuing in effective action.

Another wide field of teaching is attempted in instructing youth in the complicated process of growing up. Good books, discussion clubs, and wise counselors are enabling young people to achieve a sound adult mentality. Youth is being helped to develop the right attitude between men and women, to discover the meaning, the beauty, and the power of sex, to attain that measure of training that will insure self-support, and to develop an adequate philosophy of life capable of bearing the burdens of advancing years.

Still another line of teaching embraces an ordered body of philosophical thought dealing directly with God, Jesus, the operation of the Holy Spirit, the Church, the problem of evil, the problem of good, the Sacraments, prayer, man and his place in the world, personal salvation, social salvation, and the world mission of Christendom. This is one of the most critical needs of Christian people and of civilization itself.

The wise clergyman does not attempt to be an authority upon all fields. He brings in others who can aid—psychiatrists, doctors, parents, school teachers, lawyers, business men, nurses, and social workers. Together they help resolve personal problems, defeat habits, reduce family friction, as well as to give advice on the great issues of our day—spiritual illiteracy, secularism, commercialized amusements, liquor, national defense, war, the problems of capital, and labor.

In its teaching function the Church and its servants naturally cannot give an answer to every problem, to solve every dispute, to wipe out slums, to remove every tension or to remedy every sin of man or of society; nevertheless, they are doing much to create an atmosphere in which these problems can be solved. They are attempting to take the great issues of our day and to put them upon the conscience of mankind. There is hardly a major denomination today that has not some excellent news service, some social service commission that is providing material for discussion and reflection. The Federal Council of Churches has done a great work through its Information Service. There is no other human group so free to teach the truth in any contested areas as the clergy and members of the Christian Church. Some fail to avail themselves of this freedom—but a rather gallant lot of men and women are doing so with great effectiveness.

C. The Figure of the Healer

There are still many wounded physically and mentally beside the highways of the world; there are still many broken hearted in every parish. There are many sick and in prison. The Church has had an honorable history in the art of healing. For centuries its hostels were centers of health and mercy. In the Christian West there is hardly a major hospital that was not founded by the sacrificial gifts of some Christian group. Much of our hospitalization is now cared for by organizations with slight connection with the Church, although the hospitals had their origin there.

Within the local parish there is much that can and is being done to carry on the healing function of the Church. There are many situations in which ministers and doctors work in close collaboration.[1] As a clergyman I visit our local hospital, and day after day go into the homes where there is illness. Often I am called by doctors to talk with patients, to pray with them before operations or in crises. One comes to a family in such an hour not as a private individual but as a servant of the Church, and wholly beyond one's own merits; one carries a measure of help that is really the outgoing of the whole Church to families in distress.

As an ordinary minister I have heard confessions ranging all the way from mere peccadilloes to arson, rape, murder, sadism, plagiarism, and theft. Where the nettle of life bites deepest in shattered lives and threatened homes, in wounded children and cynical parents, in egotistical husbands and in nagging wives, the Church through its servants stands as a healer.

---

[1] A magnificent treatment of this subject may be found in *The Art of Ministering to the Sick*, by Richard C. Cabot, M.D., and Russell L. Dicks, B.D., New York, 1936.

D. The Figure of the Shepherd

Whatever else the Church is in action, as a group and through its servants and as individual members, it must bear the image of the Good Shepherd. To students upset by courses of study, to friends in prison, to those in need of blood transfusions or the spiritual communication of ideas, it can steady the mind of men. There are hosts of people who are frightened, who are out of work, who have lost confidence, who are ill or bewildered, or who rest beneath the tyranny of another's will. There are many indifferent, whose dreams of service have faded out, many who are worn to dullness by sheer fatigue—to many such the Church comes as a shepherd to protect, to encourage, and to guide.

There is a phrase I learned on the desert of southern Idaho, when herding sheep, that often comes as a reminder of my duty: "They who lead the flock must fight the wolf." The wolf comes in many guises to injure the bodies, the minds, and the souls of the people in any parish. The minister himself is not immune from these perils; he must find his help where he can. In season and out of season he must seek to substitute the realities of God in Christ, of honesty, purity, generosity, and love for their opposites. He must guard and defend the intellectual life of his community. He must not fly the agony of thought for the easier ways of action. He must meet and overcome mythologies that have become the bread and wine of so much of contemporary society, power, money, fame, totalitarian statehood. He must stand by the doctor in fighting disease; he must assist the public and private school in combating ignorance; he must attend many committee meetings of various philanthropic agencies; he must help in the hard, pedestrian work of raising money that health campaigns and milk funds and visiting nurse service shall not lack. He must seek to make persuasive, compelling, and beautiful the life of the Spirit as exemplified in Jesus Christ and in many other noble sons and daughters of God, so that the souls of his flock shall not become fat or dull or mediocre. "He who leads the flock must fight the wolf."

He must stand beside a boy who had intended to be a surgeon whose right hand is cut off by accident. He must steady that boy, encourage him to a useful life; he must help him to prepare for a different career. He must wait beside a man who has lost his eyes, and, with no foolish words of cheap sympathy, he must help him to find a long, hard road to another life of self-support and of value.

He must counsel scores of families about the higher education of their children. He must sit and listen to the hard words and harder accusations of wives and husbands, and hear bitter words of children accusing careless fathers and mothers. He must see that men and women who work at nights or at odd hours have a chance for some adequate spiritual expression of their lives. He must encourage good citizens to see the necessity for playing fields for little children in neglected quarters of the city. He must assist in providing adequate expert care in mental hygiene for children and adults in need of such service. He must not be afraid to risk his position or his reputation in facing the corrupt politician, the labor racketeer, the greedy employer, the false professional colleague. He must be willing, if he has forsaken the ideals of his profession, to leave that profession forever. He must be willing to serve a long life in what others might consider a drab parish. He must humbly, patiently, and graciously give himself to the will of God, to do out the duty, and to flash the word God gives him back to man. He and his parishioners must take unto themselves the spiritual personification of the Good Shepherd.

The practical modern asks himself, what shall I do about the Church? Shall I reject it, shall I be indifferent, shall I join it?

One can scrutinize the Church's nature and history. One can appraise by fair historical judgment the spiritual fidelity and the practical usefulness of the Church as an institution unique within the varied groupings to which men give themselves.

Or one can join a local church or parish fellowship. Certainly there is no need to stay permanently in the communion or congregation in which one is born if another is basically more congenial. Is it not reasonable to choose a church congruous to one's own nature? Within the diversity in unity that makes up the total fabric of the Christian Church, there is a wide choice not only in faith and order, but in life and work.

And one can in every manner possible live in brotherly fashion with men of other sections of the Christian Church, seeking to understand them, willing to give or to receive further light upon our common faith. The scandalous divisions among Protestant sections await a love and a faith so deep that small differences and affronts, or even large ones, will cause no split or prevent any movement toward reunion. In regard to the differences between Catholic and Protestant, owing to beliefs sincerely held by both groups, certainly no easy solution is in sight. Reunion is a long way off, or it may never come. But this is sure—if Catholics and Protestants carry themselves as Christian men, they will find help from one another and mutually encourage one another in personal piety and social action.

By prayer, by sharing of treasure and of thought, by serving the Lord of Life in and with other lives, one gradually develops the sense of Christendom, a worldview beneath the leadership of Christ. In losing one's life in service with such a group we experience the paradox of finding it in fresh insights, in renewed understanding of fellow mortals. In "endeavoring to keep the unity of the Spirit in the bond of peace," we discover "one Lord, one faith, one baptism, one God and Father of all, who is above all, and through all, and in you all."

A part of the Church's life awaits its fulfilment until it receives the loyalty, even of you and me.

Thousands of young men and women ask the question, Why should I attend Church? That question should be answered fairly, and in good spirit. Well, why should I?

Because I can thus show my loyalty to Jesus Christ upon whose life and teaching the Church is based.

Because I join in a fellowship which in origin and nature is different from all other human groups.

Because I enter into an historic unity partaking of the inherited tradition and experience of seekers and discoverers of every age, a unity based upon faith in Jesus Christ.

Because even I may contribute something to make the Church more sensitive, intelligent, and courageous.

Because I reject perfectionism as a refuge unworthy of a mature person and refuse to sit forever on the sidelines waiting for a perfect clergyman in a perfect Church in a perfect neighborhood.

Because, after scrutiny, I know no other human institution which meets so many of my needs and the needs of my family and neighbors.

Because I believe that only in company with others can I understand the full meaning of God, Jesus Christ and of the guidance of the Holy Spirit for character and career.

Because the Church offers a unique laboratory in which to investigate the bearing of Christian ethics upon contemporary problems.

Because it can, as no other body or individual, lay human need upon the conscience of mankind.

Because it can give more encouragement to prophetic spirits than any other association.

Because it can spiritualize the basic stuff of human nature, turning ancient instincts to valuable social usage.

Because in its recurrent services and sacraments I find renewal, a burnishing up of my loyalties, a casting off of prejudice and sin, and fresh strength from the living God.

Because it stirs me to creative action, shames my cowardice, lightens my sorrow, and purifies my ambition.

Because the Church gives me the most adequate idea I have yet received of human destiny.

Because in the atmosphere of fellow seekers I am best able to sort over the values life presents and to choose the higher.

Because it has been the mother of education, of healing and of science, and, in spite of ugly reversions to narrowness, and even when most colleges and hospitals are now secularized, it still draws man's responsibility to God sharply before him.

Because I, and nearly all others in the community, utilize the Church at several times in our lives, I do not wish to be parasitic.

Because the Church in a unique way is charged with the

preaching of the Gospel which for me is the supreme rule
of faith and practice.

Because I believe the Gospel is true, and therefore is true for
all men.

Because the Church alone is concerned in a major way in
sharing the Gospel in its entirety with all men.

Because the Church, because of its origin, must bring a
critique to all of life.

Because, together with the state it is a divinely ordained institution, supreme in its own moral and spiritual area.

Because the Church is the eternal "Body of Christ," and in
dignity and personality of man from encroachment from
any source.

Because the Church is the eternal "Body of Christ," and in
spite of its human weaknesses man can there find God.

SELECTED BIBLIOGRAPHY

Adam, Karl. *The Spirit of Catholicism*. Macmillan, New York, 1935. $1.50.

Bacon, Benjamin Wisner. *The Founding of the Church*. New York, 1909.

Barry, F. R. *The Relevance of the Church*. Scribner, New York, 1936. $2.50.

Bevan, Edwyn. *Christianity*. Thornton Butterworth, Ltd., London, 1932. 55 cents.

Brown, William Adams. *The Church, Catholic and Protestant*. Scribner, New York, 1935. $2.75.

_____*Church and State in Contemporary America*. Scribner, New York, 1936. $2.75.

Dodd, C. H. *The Apostolic Preaching and Its Developments*. Hodder and Stoughton, London, 1936. $1.50.

Douglass, H. P., and Brunner, E. deS. *The Protestant Church as a Social Institution*. Harper, New York, 1935. $2.50.

Hatch, Edwin. *The Organization of the Early Christian Churches*. Longmans, New York, 1909. $3.00.

Johnson, F. Ernest. *The Church and Society*. Abingdon, New York, 1935. $1.50.

Keller, Adolf. *Church and State on the European Continent*. Willett, Clark, Chicago, 1936. $2.50.

Kidd, B. J. *Documents Illustrative of the History of the Church*. 2 vols. Macmillan, New York, 1920-1923. Vol. I to A.D. 313, $2.60; Vol. II, 313-461 A.D., $3.50.

_____*History of the Church to A.D. 461*. 3 vols. Oxford, 1922. $19.35.

Lietzmann, Hans. *The Beginnings of the Christian Church*. Scribner, New York, 1937. $4.00.

Loisy, Alfred. *The Gospel and the Church*. Scribner, New York, 1913. $1.75.

Lyman, Mary Ely. *The Christian Epic*. Scribner, New York, 1936. $2.50.

Macfarland, Charles S. *Christian Unity in Practical Prophecy*. Macmillan, New York, 1933. $2.75.

McGiffert, Arthur Cushman. *A History of Christianity in the Apostolic Age*. Scribner, New York, 1920. $3.50.

More, Paul Elmer. *The Catholic Faith*. Princeton University Press, Princeton, 1931. $4.00.

Niebuhr, H. Richard. *The Social Sources of Denominationalism*. Holt, New York, 1929. $2.50.

Oldham, J. H. *The Church in the Light of the Oxford Conference*. London, 1936. $1.90.

Oman, John. *Concerning the Ministry*. Student Christian Press. London, 1936. $1.90.

Oxford Conference. *Message and Decisions on Church, Community and State*. New York, 1937. 25 cents.

Shotwell, James T., and Loomis, Louise Ropes. *The See of Peter*. Columbia University Press, New York, 1927. $10.00.

Streeter, B. H. *The Primitive Church*. Macmillan, New York, 1929. $2.50.

Temple, William. *The Church and Its Teaching Today*. Macmillan, New York, 1936. $1.00.

——————*Christ in His Church*. Macmillan, New York, 1925. $1.40.

Troeltsch, Ernst. *Social Teaching of the Christian Church*. 2 vols. Macmillan, New York, 1931. $10.50.